Bibliographic information published by the German National Library:

The German National Library lists this publication in the National Bibliography; detailed bibliographic data are available on the Internet at http://dnb.dnb.de .

Imprint:

Print and binding: Books on Demand GmbH, Norderstedt Germany
ISBN: 9783668638761

This book at GRIN:

https://www.grin.com/document/388671

Mashood Hassan

Security and Internet of Things (IoT). Analysing the difference between Austria and India in consumer awareness of IoT Vulnerabilities, perception towards IoT Privacy and Value

GRIN Verlag

Security and Internet of Things (IoT): Analysing the difference between Austria and India in consumer awareness of IoT Vulnerabilities, perception towards IoT Privacy and Value

Submitted at:

Business in Emerging Markets

(Master)

Mashood HASSAN

September 2017

Contents

Abstract

The vision of internet of things (IoT) has become a reality and in recent years, it has seen rapid growth. However, there is a lot more to come from this technological Tsunami. In simple terms, Internet of Things is a network of interconnected objects or things with sensors, collecting data and making actionable decisions. With the arrival and adaptation of this technology, many questions regarding cyber security are raised. This master thesis examines the consumer perspective on key elements of the internet of things. The elements in focus are consumer awareness, the perception of privacy and perception of value. The relationship of these elements with Gender and Nationality is investigated. The study is based on the survey of respondents belonging to Austria and India. After interviewing two experts from the field of the internet of things and reviewing the literature, the vulnerabilities surrounding IoT were confirmed. Lack of consumer awareness is considered a hindrance in the adaptation of IoT, whereas the trust between technology and consumers has decreased over time. It is claimed that consumers do not value security enough to pay extra for it.

However, the findings from this study suggest a shift in the understanding and attitude of the consumer base. The author finds while certain trends from previous researchers remain unchanged. There has been an increased awareness among consumers overall. Gender influences the awareness; value perception of consumers is also influenced by Gender and Nationality. The perception of privacy is negative, and the trust of consumers remains low. Most people would like to see more work done by the industry and the government to increase consumer education regarding cybersecurity and Internet of Things.

Keywords: Internet of Things, Security, Consumer, Awareness, Privacy, Value, Perception, Austria, India, Gender

Acknowledgement

I would first like to thank my thesis advisor Mag. DR. Rupert Beinhauer at FH Joanneum University of Applied Sciences. Prof. Beinhauer always had an open door to his office whenever I ran into trouble or had a question about my research or writing. He constantly permitted this paper to be my own work but navigated me in the right path whenever he thought I needed it.

I would especially like to thank the two experts for taking out time for the interviews and for their valuable input. DI (FH) Michael Brickmann MA who is a Full Professor at the FH Joanneum in Graz, Austria and Prof. Marko Bajec who is a Full Professor at the Faculty of Computer & Information Science, University of Ljubljana. This thesis could not have been possible without their input and expertise.

Finally, I must express my profound gratitude to my parents Zahid Hassan Qureshi and Rubeena Zahid for providing me with constant support and nonstop encouragement throughout my years of education. This accomplishment would not have been possible without them.

Thank you!

Mashood Hassan

List of Abbreviations

IoT: Internet of Things

ISACA: Information Systems Audit and Control Association

ESET: Executive Security and Engineering Technologies

VPN: Virtual Private Network

List of Figures

List of Tables

1) Introduction

This master thesis explored three areas that are crucial to a more secure adaptation of Internet of Things in the coming years. These areas include consumer awareness, perception of privacy and perception of value. With Internet of Things devices and application already becoming popular consumer purchases, the prospects from the industry look very promising, in the case of profitability and growth. However, Internet of Things has also brought with it question marks over the security of networks and the privacy of its users. These questions need to be answered to help build confidence in the industry and gain consumer trust. The author will explore distinct aspects on the consumer side which will bring forward their perspective. Also, to highlight if major gaps exist between the industry and the consumers. The thesis is divided into three phases, the first phase looks at the literature to find out and understand the security vulnerabilities of Internet of Things and what are some of the core challenges that the industry is faced with concerning awareness, privacy and understanding the value perception of consumers. The second phase of thesis will include interviews with experts and a survey of the population from the selected countries. In the third and final phase of the thesis, author will present a conclusion, giving recommendations of the findings and a brief comment of the implications for future research.

In the past 10-15 years, wireless communication systems have grown rapidly. Today we have RFID, Wi-Fi, 4G and what not! All of this has helped the internet of things to become what it is today. These technologies have especially been useful for driving smart monitoring and controlling applications. Presently, the concept of IoT has many sides, it holds many diverse technologies, services and standards. But with this elevated level of heterogeneity and a wide scale of systems, security threats associated with the current Internet are expected to magnify and take new forms. (Sicari, Rizzardi, Grieco, & Coen-Porisini, 2014)

The concepts of controlling, revealing and hiding our privacy has evolved with the changing face of technology and data use. In the recent era, connection to the Internet was cautious, optional, autonomous and most importantly consensual. Entering the new world of data collection of sensors all around us, our physical environments, the smartphones inside the pockets, appliances in our homes, smart-cars etc in the world of Internet of Things, there is no shutting down the laptop and just walking away. As the interactions of consumer with digital technology changes from the laptop into this physical world, so must the transparency of these interactions. (Groopman, 2015) Taking everything into context, it is now more than ever the need to time for consumer to be on the page as the industry and stop taking security for granted.

1.1) Research Motivation and Purpose

Internet of Things is a phenomenon that will be experiencing rapid growth in the coming years and by 2020 it is expected to add $20 trillion to the global economy. (Manyika, et al., 2015) The author as a consumer himself of IoT products was fascinated with the idea of doing research on consumers, to gauge the level of their understanding and alertness to this gigantic technological tsunami that is building up slowly but surely.

Problem Statement: To analyse the difference between Austrian and Indian consumers with regards to awareness of IoT Vulnerabilities, perception towards Privacy and Value.

Cyber Security Incidents

To highlight the importance of the topic and its relevance in present times, below some of the major news developments and incidents are mentioned that have taken place around the time of conception of this study.

- **Petya ransomware attack:** Numerous organizations in the US and in EU have been sabotaged by a ransomware attack known as Petya. The malicious software spread through large firms leading to PCs and data being locked up and held for ransom. Firms such as WPP (advertiser), food company Mondelez, DLA Piper (legal firm) and Maersk (Danish shipping and transport firm) were compromised. (Solon & Hern, 2017)

- **Russians hack the DNC**: Arguably, the biggest news to come out in the previous year with regards to cyber security was the American Elections and the acquisition of the U.S. towards Russia of hacking the democratic party and influencing the result of the elections. This made worldwide news and forced people to think about cyber warfare in the years to come. (BBC, 2017)
- **From Britain to India, massive ransomware attack creates havoc:** The Britain's National Cyber Security Centre teams had their work cut out in restoring hospital computer systems after a global cyber-attack hit various countries including the UK and India. UK suffered an attack on its NHS, this lead to forced closures of British hospitals to cancel and delay treatment for patients. (hindustantimes, 2017)
- **Attack on internet infrastructure provider Dyn:** A symbol of 2016 cyber-attacks has been just how public they have become. In October, an attack on internet infrastructure provider Dyn tool place and a "distributed denial of service (DDoS) attack" (Wheelwright, 2016) took down access to Netflix, Facebook, Twitter plus the Guardian, CNN, the New York Times, the Wall Street Journal and others.

1.2) Previous research done on Internet of Things

To help develop a good understanding of and gain insight into previous research, the literature sources available are divided into three categories, primary (published and unpublished), secondary and tertiary. These categories also incline to frequently overlap: for example, primary literature sources, including conference proceedings, can appear in journals, and some books contain indexes to primary and secondary literature. Altogether, the distinct groups of literature resources epitomise the flow of information from the original source. Often as information flows from the primary to secondary and then to tertiary sources, it grows into less detail and decreased authoritativeness but is more easily accessible. (Saunders, Lewis, & Thornhill, 2009)

Until a few years ago, Internet of things was still an emerging phenomenon but now it has truly come into the lime light and there have been numerous studies conducted on it. The research done has been varied in its perspectives and covers a vast number of issues concerning with the IoT. However, the most notable research conducted are the survey "The Internet of Things: Future of Consumer Adoption" by Accenture from the acquity international group (Accenture, 2014) and "Unlocking the potential of Internet of things" by McKinsey Global Institute.

The Accenture survey which was study of 2000 consumers across the U.S and focused on consumer adoptions and tried to examine their preferences and behaviour with regards to Internet of things and connected technology. While the McKinsey report focused on discussing the value that would be offered by the potential products and services of Internet of Things.

A major research report "Harnessing IoT Global Development" (Biggs, Garrity, LaSalle, & Polomska, 2016) was presented to the UN Broadband Commission for Sustainable Development. Apart from the mentioned studies various other researches has been done in the fields of cyber security and Internet of Things, which were toughly reviewed and are occasionally referenced in this Master Thesis as well.

1.3) Research Gap (How is this study different?)

The research conducted on the topic of Internet of Things in the years gone by has mostly focused on adaptation of the technology and highlighting the value perceived and value offered by it, meaning answering questions like What do consumers want from IoT technology, identifying the desires of consumers or focusing on Value offering, the type of services and products that would be most valuable on the market. Although, the aspect of cyber security has indeed been highlighted in the literature, no study has been conducted focusing on the consumer awareness, perception of privacy and perception of value for India and Austria. This study will talk about the other side of the equation, what if the internet of things and the technology associated with it was to fall into the wrong hands? Are consumers aware of possibilities security breaches or prepared for it? How do the handle privacy? Would they value security in monetary terms? What segments of IoT are most popular among them?

The interviews of the experts conducted in this Master Thesis highlight the security issues faced by the adaptation of Internet of Things and then the interview findings lead up to the creating of the survey done on the population. Researchers have highlighted the security threats posed by the internet of things, but the consumer perspective has been overlooked to an extent, this leaves a black hole in the industry as to the understanding of the IoT technology by an average consumer. And thus far, no research was carried out to see if the gender or nationality of the consumer influences in their idea and understanding of IoT.

1.4) Choice of Countries

India

Reviewing the literature, it became clear that adoption of Internet of Things is on a constant rise across several industries in India. Moreover, with the Indian Government also keen to develop many smart cities, IoT would be used in various applications such as smart lighting, smart parking and solid waste management. It is anticipated that an increased need for connectivity among devices to automate business processes and for instantaneous monitoring/tracking Internet of Things will further drive India's market through 2022. Moreover, with regards to associated communication technology, short range communication technology earned the highest-share in Indian IoT market for 2016, this trend is likely to continue during the forecasted period till 2022. The major end users of

IoT technology in the country include Consumer Electronics, Automotive & Transportation, Energy and Utilities, with all the four end use segments seizing a majority value share in the country's Internet of Things market in the previous year of 2016. (PRNewswire, 2017)

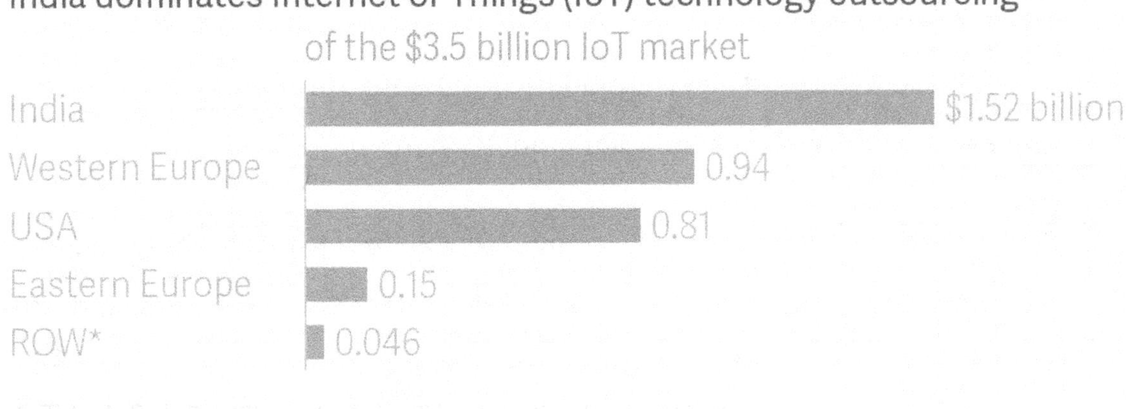

Figure 1 Quartz India Report (Bhattacharya, 2017)

In the chart above, Indian based companies are already dominating the Internet of things market, so the adaptation is quite far ahead. “Companies like Tata Consultancy Services (TCS), HCL Technologies, Wipro, Infosys, and Tech Mahindra are listed among the established and expansive market leaders in the IoT space.” (Bhattacharya, 2017)

These companies will most likely advance as the worldwide IoT associated products and services expenditure is anticipated to increase. Nonetheless, while this technology is anticipated to generate 25,000 jobs by 2021, on the flipside it is also expected to eliminate 94,000 of them thereby adding on to the problem of downsizings associated to automation. (Bhattacharya, 2017)

Austria

Much like India, a lot of work is being done on Internet of things adaptation in Austria. Although most of this work/research in being conducted for the companies, to bring about innovation in business processes and automation. However, there is also a keen interest in developing consumer-oriented products with people like Frank Riemensperger at the forefront. The Chairman of the Accenture Management Board for Germany, Austria, Switzerland, emphasized in his keynote: "It is the experience associated with a product that makes the actual change." (Frick, 2016)

The choice of selected countries was made because of the authors interest in the Austrian consumers of Internet of Things compared with the consumers in India which is regarded to be ahead of most countries in IoT enabled consumer maturity. (Computer, 2017)

Besides that, India is an IT hub and has vastly different dynamics with regards to size, demographics and economy compared to Austria, in this context the author was interested to research about the possible difference in the outcome regarding consumer awareness of IoT vulnerabilities, perception of privacy and value perceived for different IoT segments. Moreover, no previous research of such scale has been conducted with regards to the selected countries and the response of consumers on the topic was of keen interest to the author.

1.5) Gender

The previous research done on the topic suggests a difference in the perspectives of Genders when it comes to adoption of the technology. According to (Accenture, 2014) research done on U.S consumers, genders differed with self-identifying their technology habits. This included innovators, early adopters, mass consumers, late adopters and consumers who planned to never use IoT technology. The report points out that, men were twice as more likely to be aware of the term Internet of things (IoT) and consider themselves to be early adopters of the technology. As compared to women, men are more likely to have owned or plan to purchase devices using Internet of Things (IoT) Technology.

Furthermore, the study (Accenture, 2014) suggests that in the case of sharing of data from connected devices, men and women differentiate in terms of the service being offered in return for the information they provide. For instance, women show to be slightly more likely than men (54% vs 47%) to share data from a connected car in return for location-based coupons or similar discounts. Men whereas, are more likely (33% vs 22%) to share data from a connected car if informed of possibly interesting places along their route.

1.6) Expected Outcome

With this thesis, the author investigates three key elements which are crucial to the realization of the Internet of Things. These key three elements are; Consumer Awareness; Perception of Privacy and Perception of Value.

By analysing Consumer Awareness, the idea is to highlight the gaps that exist between the industry and the consumer. By "gap" the author means, the lack of awareness regarding the general idea of what IoT is and IoT vulnerabilities, not the technical aspects of the IoT devices and applications. The results from this analysis should be beneficial in understanding consumer behaviour and awareness towards IoT, which can then be used by companies to create better communication channels and relationships with consumers.

The second element of IoT to be examined is the Consumer Perception of Privacy with regards to the Internet of Things. In the coming years, consumer trust will be a very important indicator of how much the public is open towards a mass adaptation of IoT in a society. With the results from analysing this variable, it would be possible to judge, to some extent at least, where the consumers stand with regards to privacy about IoT devices and application. Either they will have a positive perception, which would make things easier for IoT implementation, or they have a negative perception in which case this can be another opportunity for the industry to address these concerns.

Consumer Perception of Value is the third variable to be highlighted and analysed by the author. This variable is particularly important as its outcome will reveal in what capacity do consumers seek value within the realm of Internet of Things, what type of products they are more interested in and how much are they willing to pay for security and privacy. It will point out, where consumers are willing to spend money or even pay more in certain respects. To explore the behaviour of consumers with regards to their value perception of IoT products and applications. This could be very useful for the industry going forward, as it can help companies devise their strategy for sales with regards to Gender and Nationality.

The purpose of thesis is to help bridge the gap between the industry and consumer. To help understand where the consumers understanding is of the technology and where more effort can be made to help increase the understanding to have a safer, more prosperous co-existence of technology and society as we know it.

In the end, a comparison will be made between the consumers of the two selected countries i.e. Austria and India and between the two Genders, to highlight difference/similarities.

2) What is Internet of Things?

The era of Internet of Things seems to be upon us, yet people are not as familiar with the term as they should be. To put it in simple terms the whole idea of IoT is, 'A worldwide network of interconnected entities'. (Roman, Zhou, & Lopez, 2013) To have an interconnected and cooperative digital environment using smart technology evolving the current internet infrastructure is what the Internet of Things model envisages. On the path of evolution, it will end up aiding many innovative services that will be improving the everyday lives of ordinary people, brood new businesses, make smart buildings, cities, and transport. (Ziegeldorf, Morchon, & Wehrle, Privacy in the Internet of Things: threats, 2013)

In its idea, the internet of things is vast, full of endless possibilities and exciting for the technologically enriched society that it promises to give. When we talk about IoT, we are talking about many smart devices, all of which are interacting with each other and collaborating in accomplishing a common goal. It is a sharing environment like never, taking cloud technology to new heights. IoT finds application in many different fields, for example: patients remote monitoring, energy consumption control, traffic control, smart parking system, inventory management, production process, the customization of shopping at supermarkets and the protection for public. (Sicari, Rizzardi, Grieco, & Coen-Porisini, 2014)

To develop a picture of how IoT works, imagine a world consisting of many devices that you are surrounded by and they can all communicate, sense and share information, at the same time, all are interconnected over a public or private cloud. Now these devices simultaneously collect data regularly, analyse it and use it to perform an action, providing substantial amounts of intelligent data for management, planning and decision making. This sums up the reality of the Internet of Things.

2.1) Economic Impact

The Internet of Things is not just having a social impact, economically it is going to be huge as well. It is growing swiftly, in 2011 the overall number of interconnected devices present on the planet overtook the actual number of people. However, the projection is of 25 billion connected 'things' throughout the globe by 2020. While the, added value from the Internet of Things is projected to be worth US$1.9 trillion by the same year, proving its economic significance. (Davies, 2015)

The biggest growth in terms of money should come from factories which could be explained by the increasing automation and the replacement of low level workers by machines. Growth in Cities is already visible, with the idea of Smart Cities becoming popular. There is also significant growth potential in Retail, Automotive and logistics segments. The human segment of the IoT is what this thesis would be focusing on. The third section of the survey is devoted to value perception of the consumer, which should help identify where the value lies within the Human segment of the Internet of Things. The image below forecasts the economic impact of the internet of things technology, highlighting the important segments with their prospective growth. On a side note, it is important to keep in mind that the data in the image is from 2015, which will make it interesting later, to see if there have been any changes in the past two years. Moreover, it will also be interesting to find out the economic impact on Austria and Indian in specific. To develop a "Big Picture" of the Internet of Things the following image perfectly sums up how most sections of society will have to incorporate this technology moving forward.

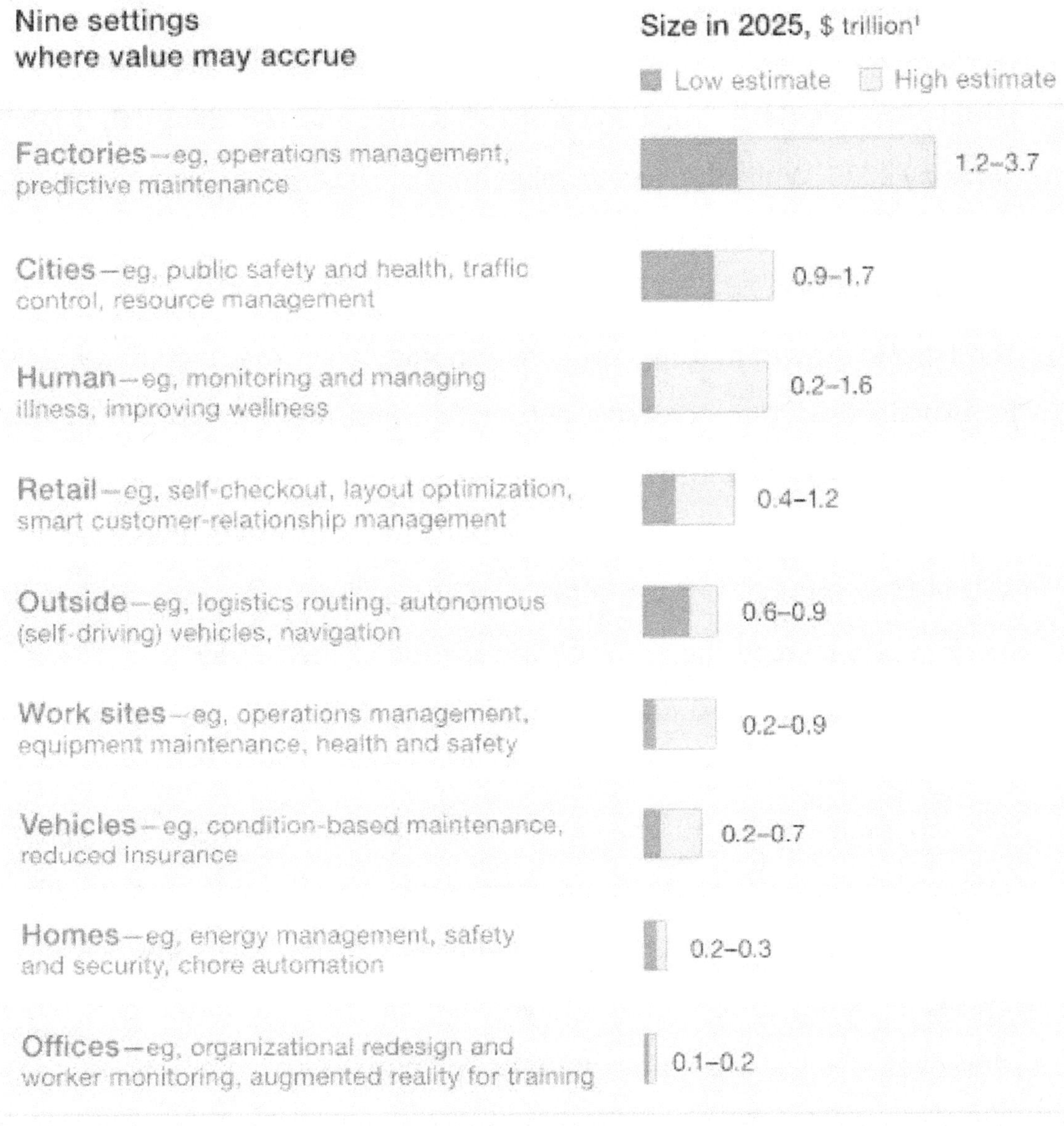

Figure 2 Economic Impact of IoT (James Manyika, 2015)

2.2) Internet of Things Segments

IoT Analytics – *Quantifying the connected world*

Internet of Things – Market segmentation by industry/application

Global level: IoT world market

Customer type:
- 1 Consumer-facing (IoT2C)
- 2 Business-facing (IoT2B)

Main category	Industries/applications
1a Home	• Home automation • Home improvement • Energy efficiency
1b Lifestyle	• Wearable computing • Entertain-ment & Music • Family • Leisure • Pets • Toys • Drones
1c Health	• Fitness • Monitoring • Measurement • Diagnosis
1d Mobility	• Connected cars • eBikes
2a Retail	• Stores • Shops • Convenience
2b Health	• Monitoring • Measurement • Diagnosis • Surgery • Patient care
2c Energy	• Transmission& Distribution • Fossil • Nuclear • Alternative
2d Mobility	• Aerospace& Airports • Marine • Rail&Stations • Automotive • Traffic
2e Cities	• Infrastructure • Water/ Wastewater • HVAC • Lighting • Security • Life safety
2f Manufact.	• Mining • Oil&Gas • Discrete production • Contin. Production • Supply Chain
2g Public& Services	• Schools • Universities • Government • Banking • Insurance • Admin-istration • Commercial services
2h Other	• Environment • Military • Agriculture • Hospitality

We consider the following applications as adjacent to the Internet of Things but not part of it: Car sharing, ePayment

For more information, go to www.iot-analytics.com © IoT-Analytics.com 2014. All rights reserved.

Figure 3. IoT segments (Lueth, IoT market segments – Biggest opportunities in industrial manufacturing, 2014)

In the Image above, we can see the distribution of IoT in various segments. Whether it is for Businesses or Consumers, IoT will influence almost all fields of life. Companies must come up with new strategies to incorporate IoT and make sure they do not miss out of the revolutionary phase of technology, whereas they also should rethink their marketing strategies and build new relationships with consumers. Enterprises will also have room to grow, IoT brings to the table some concrete business benefits such as improved management, better tracing of assets and products, innovative/evolving business models and a chance to achieve cost saving through the optimized use of resources.

In this thesis, the focus was on the consumer side, to find out the knowledge and standing of consumers, specifically from Austria and India on three core aspects relating to the technology, i.e. Awareness, Perception of Privacy and Perception of Value. With the growing number of smart devices coupled with other physical objects connected within the Internet of Things network, the influence and value it brings to our daily lives is becoming more prevalent as well. People get to make better informed decisions, for instance, taking the best route to work or picking their favourite restaurant, with ease like never. Modern technology can pave way for modern services to emerge as an answer to the challenges of the society. A Remote health monitoring system for elderly patients and pay as you use services can be taken as examples in this regard. As for the government, the merging of the data sources on the shared networks improves nationwide planning, increases harmony between agencies and most of all facilitating faster responsiveness to emergencies or disasters (LLP, 2011)

2.3) Growth

No longer Internet of Things can be called an emerging phenomenon. It is well and truly here; many consumers already own or are planning to buy in home IoT devices. As IoT will increase the synergy between the real and the digital world, the volume of data that is collected by sensors will be considerably larger than in the current Internet technology and the data will be more detailed and associated with the daily activities of the citizens. Which means going forward the influence of IoT on our daily lives is only likely to grow. With the recent advances in sensing technologies, social networking and mobile and cloud technologies, the boundaries between the physical, social, and cyber worlds have been blurred out. Leading to the astounding growth of internet users (from 1.158 billion in 2007 to 3 billion in 2014) and growth of internet connected devices (to 15 billion in 2014). The result has been an explosion of data produced from a myriad of internet connected devices and social networks. (BERTINO, CHOO, GEORGAKOPOLOUS, & NEPAL, 2016)

In the previous section we have already discussed the rapid rise of IoT. But, if we are to talk about the different segments of IoT, then it seems Health and Fitness will be the most popular, with many people already owning wearable devices, this segment is expected to flourish. While there is also a keen trend towards the purchase of home appliances. To help understand this phenomenal growth rate and potential of internet of things we should know about the contributing factors which have provided a boost to Internet of Things adoption.

- The decrease in expense of computing in part with the evolution of Wi-Fi are empowering factors in the growth of IoT applications.
- Fast growth in mobile technology and the distribution of 3G networks from 2001 forwards, coupled with the increased connectivity globally including urban to rural.
- The surge of software development that is partly attributable to economies of scale is another significant contributor.

(Biggs, Garrity, LaSalle, & Polomska, 2016)

Both business and individual consumers have been open to the fact that Internet of Things devices and application are drastically improving efficiency. Which is paving way for innovation of new business models and changes in everyday behaviour of the general population.

Future Trends

Internet of Things, specifically with regards to cyber security will be the centre of attention in the coming years, with a study (Newman, 2017) predicting $1 trillion to be spent annually by 2021 on a global level. The main future course of Internet of Things development can be summarized in the following points:

- Nearly $6 trillion will be spent on it over the course of next five years.
- Businesses will be the top adopter of IoT solutions. They are three ways the IoT can improve their bottom line, by lowering operating costs, increasing productivity and expanding into new markets or developing innovative product.

- Governments are focused on growing productivity, reducing costs and improving the quality of life of citizens. They will likely be the second-largest adopters of IoT systems.
- Consumers will lag businesses and governments in IoT adoption. Still, they will be buying a vast number of devices and invest a substantial amount of money in IoT.

(Newman, 2017)

2.4) Security and Internet of Things

To quote Deloitte's Dana Spataru at the IoT Solutions World Congress in Barcelona, end October 2016: "Data is the new oil, and data leaks are the new oil spills". (Clerck)

In a research conducted by HP (Company, 2014), 10 most popular devices under the cloud of Internet of Things were reviewed. The result of the research showcased some disturbing statistics. It pointed out a high average number of susceptibilities per each of the device. The nature of the threats varied from a Heartbleed to denial of service due to weak passwords to cross-site scripting. Almost all the devices working with the Internet of things will require some sort of personal information as input. (Company, 2014) Some of these devices were said to be having weak security. While a lot of these popular devices were shown to be vulnerable to attackers and easy to identify. A summary from the results of the HP report is shown in the image below.

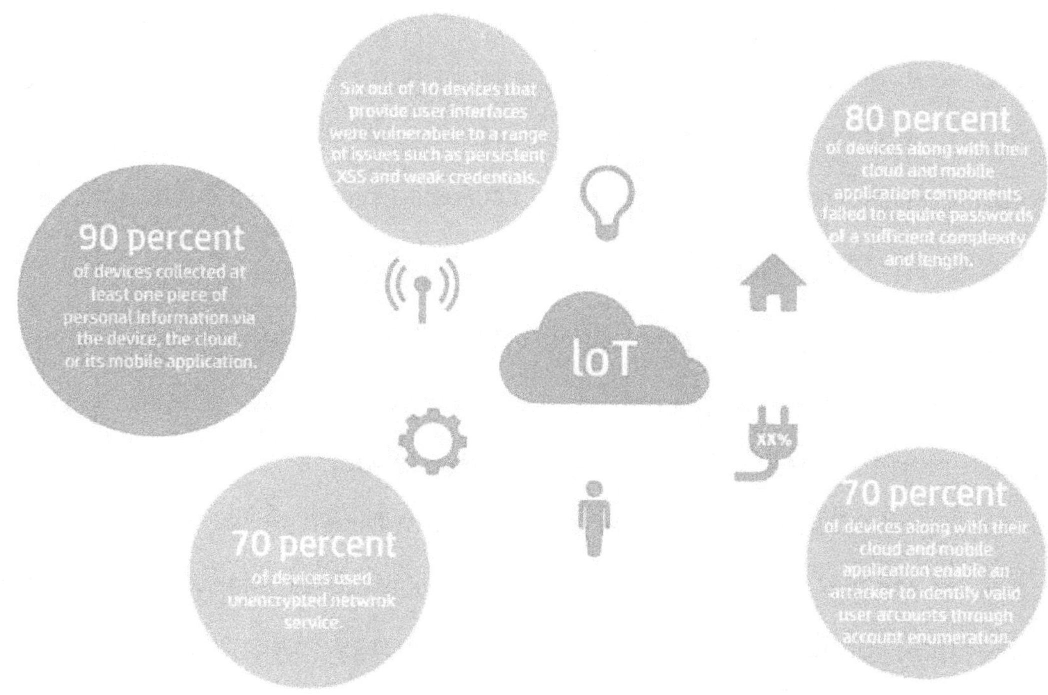

Figure 4 HP Research Findings (Company, 2014)

From the literature, the section about the security threats and vulnerabilities to Internet of Things will be highlighted the most as it forms the basis of the thesis. However, the author would like to state that the technicalities regarding the Internet of Things devices and application with not be explored in detail as they require a more thorough IT and programming qualification, which the author is not equipped with. In this section, the major security concerns according to the literature will be put forward in a simplistic manner as to be easy understandable to a lay man without in depth knowledge of IoT workings.

To put it very briefly, the concept of Internet of things means "A worldwide network of interconnected entities." Because IoT has such a vast array of devices and applications, no single strategy might be applicable to secure the vision of Internet of Things. IoT ecosystems are being designed to handle a number closer to billions of objects, that will cooperate among themselves and other diverse objects or things. These interactions must be protected in some way! Shielding the data and services running all related elements and restraining the quantity of occurrences that will affect the full IoT. (Roman, Zhou, & Lopez, 2013) The core problem of securing IoT lies in its complexity, because it's something different and new, the traditional methods of security do not apply here. "The number of attack vectors available to malicious attackers might become staggering, as global connectivity (''access anyone'') and accessibility (''access anyhow, anytime'') are key tenets of the IoT". (Roman, Zhou, & Lopez, 2013)

With the recent scandals US elections being hacked and groups like anonymous getting increasingly prominent in the mainstream media, it's safe to say that time has come to take these threats as serious. In fact, one of the problems with the security of IoT seems to be that people do not take it seriously, believing that they will never be the victims. IoT finds application in many different fields, for example; patients remote monitoring, energy consumption control, traffic control, smart parking system, inventory management, production chain, customization of shopping, civil protection. Users from these require the protection of personal information related to movements, habits and interactions with other people. In a single term, their privacy should be guaranteed. (Sicari, Rizzardi, Grieco, & Coen-Porisini, 2014)

When we raise questions about IoT security threats, there are a lot of possibilities, to understand these threats, it is first important to break-down the major areas of vulnerabilities. Some of these might seem to be overlapping but in the case of Internet of Things, as everything is under a cloud, therefore different areas are closely linked together. If one is compromised, it would probably lead to the other areas being vulnerable as well. This complexity is one more reason to understand this technology, so consumers can be better equipped to ask question of the industry personnel who are developing these devices. The major areas concerning security issues are highlighted and discussed below:

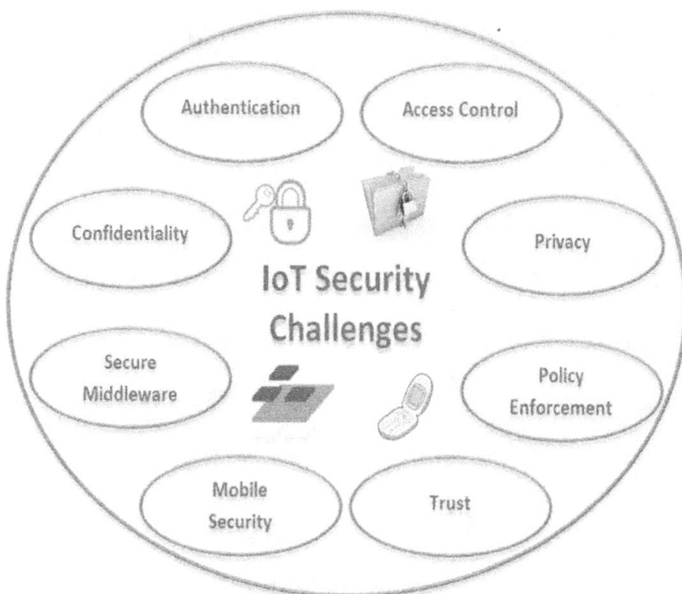

Figure 5 IoT Security Challenges (Sicari, Rizzardi, Grieco, & Coen-Porisini, 2014)

The image above shows the major security challenges that are being faced by IoT. And they have a lot to do with consumer security and privacy. The presence of billions of diverse objects makes it extremely complicated to do identity management. Authorization is another important feature closely related to authentication, if there exist no access control, all could be get into by everybody. This is neither feasible nor realistic, in fact, the data surge caused because of the mass 'things' producing information is a significant threat to the privacy. Which is why it being important for users to have the tools that would let them hold their anonymous status in this well-connected world.

The extensiveness' and variedness of the IoT does affects the trust and governance of it as well. See from a rational viewpoint, an IoT system can be described as a collection of smart devices that network on a collaborative basis to realize a common goal. Traditional security counter-measures and privacy tools cannot directly be applied to this technology due to their limited computing power. Then there is the issue of scalability cause by the sizeable number of inter-connected devices. Therefore, a flexible structure is needed to be able to handle the threats arising in such a dynamic setting. (Sicari, Rizzardi, Grieco, & Coen-Porisini, 2014)

For IoT to work, consumers should have a guarantee for data anonymity, confidentiality and integrity. There should also be better mechanisms preventing unauthorized users (i.e., humans and devices) to access the system. Collectively with the conventional security solutions, there is the need to provide built-in security for the devices (i.e., embedded) to add active prevention, discovery, diagnosis, isolation and resourceful countermeasures against breaches. IoT, as we know allows a constant transfer and sharing of data amongst things and users to achieve respective goals. In such a flowing and sharing environment, authentication, authorization, access-control and nonrepudiation are vital to safeguard secure communication. (Sicari, Rizzardi, Grieco, & Coen-Porisini, 2014) Then another non-security flaw which is rather non-technical in nature is the lack of legislative cover for consumers. And non-extant minimum set standards for the Industry.

"The rapid spread of connected devices is outpacing an organization's ability to manage it and to safeguard company and employee data." said Christos Dimitriadis who is the international president of ISACA and group director of Information Security for INTRALOT. (ISACA, ISACA Survey, 2015)

Data scientists and analysts have different views on this subject. Some are prepared to 'embrace' this Internet of Things for most of the benefits it propositions, while others are worried by it. The later, directing to the possible hazards of the networked things, believing that the rising tendency of connectivity, which has all these sensing devices and can co-operate with each another will only expand the possibility of attacks and increase vulnerabilities. Looking back, there were various prominent occasions that have shown us just how susceptible some connected devices can be to hackers. (BullGuard, 2017) Some of the examples include:

1. A connected toilet seat controlled through an Android application got hacked by researchers, which caused this toilet to continually flush, thereby, increasing the water usage.

2. Researchers exposed a fault in smart-TV programmes and launched something termed a 'red button attack'. The smart-TV data stream was hacked and then used to takeover what was shown on the screen. One ransomware hit an Android Smart TV and subsequently demanded $500.
3. Many researchers have proved how the 'smart-cars' may easily be hacked. The effects range from killing off the brakes to manoeuvring the car from left to right.
4. 'Cyber-criminals' succeeded in penetrating the sensors of a state facility and a manufacturing plant in New Jersey. Thereby, they could remotely alter the temperature inside these buildings.
5. In the US, frighteningly internet connected baby monitors have been successfully hacked. Hacker would then scream at the child to make them awake or even post video feeds of these children on the internet. (BullGuard, 2017)

Basic Security Measures purposed by literature

Technology like the Internet of Things can be difficult to understand for a common consumer with limited technical know-how. When a regular consumer buys a connectable device, the 'user manual' guides them through the basic procedure of connecting and configuring. There is very little emphasis on protecting and securing the device and the network. Most consumers don't even change the default username, password, and the wireless key of the connected devices. (MSV, 2016) And this puts them in a lot of risk, without them even knowing about it. Which is why experts purposing some basic security measure that could be used to prevent security breaches. A survey by ESET in co-operation with the National Cyber Security Alliance revealed that more than 40% are "not confident at all" in the safety and security of IoT Devices. ((NCSA) National Cyber Security Alliance & ESET , 2016)

Granted, it is hard for consumers to implement the security processes undertaken by enterprises in their datacentres, still they can apply a few best practices. There are some basic steps that could make the IoT and connected devices more secure:

1. Always change the default username and password of the device. This includes everything from the Wi-Fi router to the smart home hub.
2. Ensure that the software is up to date for all devices and connected systems (including router firmware).
3. Check whether the home security software has router protection.
4. To be informed about what data is being collected and stored by the connected devices.
5. Limiting device and/or application privileges.

2.5) Consumer awareness of IoT Vulnerabilities

In the world of Internet of Things, consumers will be surrounded by devices big and small which are always collecting data. The devices almost have a life of their own, in the way they are setup. But while they will undoubtedly contribute to raising the living standard of the society, they also possess flaws making them susceptible to threats, like hacking or identity theft. The crucial feature of Internet of things technology is the fact that it can enable communication amid two or more devices without human involvement. That's exactly why it is important to learn about the level of awareness the potential consumers have of this knowledge.

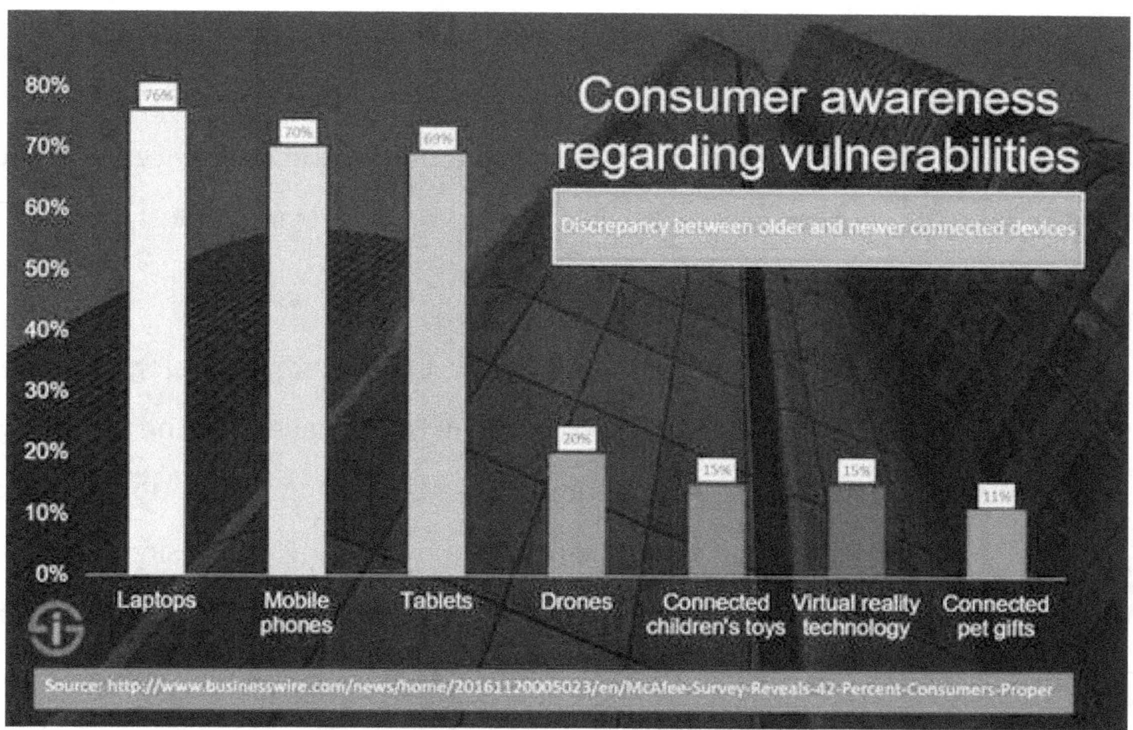

Figure 6 Awareness of IoT Devices (Security, 2016)

The author defines consumer awareness of IoT Vulnerabilities as the realization of the existence of vulnerabilities of the IoT, not the awareness about the details of the flaws or the technical aspects of the vulnerabilities themselves. In the literature, the issue of consumer awareness has been highlighted by various authors. According to the McAfee Security Reveals, most consumers are somewhat aware about the vulnerabilities associated with traditional connected devices such as laptops, Mobile phones and tablets. However, when it comes to modern technology, the consumers seem to be clueless. (Security, 2016) One major research conducted by Accenture's Acquity Group showed that consumer awareness is one of the barriers to the success of IoT. The study based of 2000 consumer surveys from the U.S, shows alarming signals. With 87% of the respondents saying they have not heard of the term "Internet of Things". (Accenture, 2014) And when it comes to awareness, it is not just the individuals that seem to be behind time, businesses appear to be having the same problem. As customers, we have developed an obsession with connected devices. Most people love the concepts of these smart-homes, smart-cars, smart-TVs, smart-refrigerators or other machines that are automated by using sensors. Yet very few other topics in IT today stir further fear than the idea of corporate networks being breached by this booming trend of hacking connected devices. The internet of things spectacle enhances this threat surface tremendously and in turn furthering business dangers. (Boulton, 2016)

For such a diverse and vast spectrum of connected technology, it is highly significant to develop a holistic security plan. But to have that, the first thing that needs to be done is consumer education. A recent report from Ubuntu indicates the 'consumer awareness campaigns' were not having the desired effect. Even went on to claim that consumers seem mostly ignorant of the intensifying threat established by the rise in IoT and cyber-attacks in 2016. (Canonical, 2017) The fact of the matter seems to be that there is tremendous work that need to be done to build up consumer awareness and trust when it comes to IoT, because not having that, security would almost be impossible.

In the previous researches, many authors seem to be making this point that, educating the people is critical in stopping security breaches. One can invest heavily in 'state of the art' security solution having predictive analytics, embedded security and whatnot! but if this 'human factor' is ignored, then nothing else works. (Weber, 2010) Another crucial factor that needs to be analysed is that correct information about the product is a 'consumer right'. The consumers should know exactly the kind of product they are purchasing. But this factor has two sides, one is the industry principle to make the information available in a clear and easily accessible way, and then it is also a responsibility of the people buying a product to make sure they try to find out at least a little bit about the security of the product. It is vital that average customers understand that they can help play a part in the fight against these attacks.

The trouble is, consumers might already own a lot of the products that are suspect but might not be aware of that. For which reason, it is important to ask questions like, how are the buying decisions being made specially when it comes to technological products. Because poor decision making can put you at risk with tech-products. Internet of Things will no doubt mould into our lives, because the growth potential is far too great to be ignored or suppressed. But before things get too far, it is imperative to highlight the impact of consumer awareness of devices on corporate networks and a hindrance to mass implementation of IoT in the future. Because, there is a lack of consumer awareness and a lack of knowledge about the value of what the Internet of things must offer. Trend seems to show a clear interest in IoT but a lack of awareness at the same time. (Lueth, IoT market segments 'Biggest opportunities in industrial manufacturing', 2014) There is a need to study factors, that could prove to be a hindrance in the optimization of IoT. Having the right knowledge regarding the level of consumer awareness can help the industry in setting up standards and identifying where the gap is when it comes to consumer knowledge of internet of things vulnerabilities.

To sum it up, IoT systems introduce many vulnerabilities as each single device represents a potential risk and is a potential attack vector. From the hardware, firmware to the applications running on these devices, these could hypothetically provide entrances for unsanctioned access. (BERTINO, CHOO, GEORGAKOPOLOUS, & NEPAL, 2016) Consumers need to have this knowledge, which could help them make better purchasing decisions or making them more secure with the products that surround them.

2.6) Perception towards Privacy

Privacy has almost been at the forefront of the discussion, when talking about technological advancement. And with the arrival of Internet of Things, we have numerous inter-connected devices, privacy invasion is a grave concern. The problem is not just the fact that there are all these devices with sensors, it is that they are collecting data and based on that, making decision FOR the individual. So, what we have now is, an efficient and smart society, with a very diverse network filled with useful information. There needs to be a balance between the rights of consumers to keep their personal data private and protected, to have the power of consent over its use, the significant benefits that can ensue to companies and society from the analysis of such a loaded data source. According to recent studies, 72% of the internet users in the EU already say they are concerned that they are being requested to share too much personal data online. (Davies, 2015) Privacy is a wide-ranging and diverse concept which is why literature is filled with several definitions and perspectives. If we take a historic interpretation, the idea of privacy has shifted amongst media, territory, communication, and physical privacy. With the growing usage and efficiency of the electronic data processing, information privacy developed into the principal issue today. Westin in 1968 defined Information privacy as "the right to select what personal information about me is known to what people." (Ziegeldorf, Morchon, & Wehrle, Privacy in the Internet of Things: threats, 2013)

"Privacy in the Internet of Things is threefold; guarantee to the subject for awareness of privacy risks imposed by smart things and services surrounding the data subject, individual control over the collection and processing of personal information by the surrounding smart things, awareness and control of subsequent use and dissemination of personal information by those entities to any entity outside the subject's personal control sphere". (Ziegeldorf, Morchon, & Wehrle, Privacy in the Internet of Things: Threats and Challenges, 2013) With the emergence of an Internet of Things, new regulatory approaches to ensure its privacy and security become necessary. The question must be addressed; How much privacy the civil society is prepared to surrender to increase security? With the digitalization of the physical world and the arrival of Internet of Things the expectations of privacy are being challenged. With the introduction of sensors to people, to objects and to places all around us makes the physical world communicable and contextual while also making it trackable. The full consequences of universal connectivity may not be fully understood or forecasted by the industry driving it, never mind the end users. (Groopman, 2015)

Figure 7 Privacy of a Device Cloud (Schneider, 2016)

Cyber security today in a data heavy digitally transformed economy, is simply critical for the successful working, conducting business and other aspects of our society. (Weber, 2010) The alarming fact about privacy is that it appears the industry is falling short of providing the bare minimum, with a survey of IT professionals suggesting that sufficient security measures are not being implemented by manufacturers of these IoT devices. While they also believe that the standards available now in the industry are not sufficient. Basic security measure such as having all the private devices within the private cloud and then protecting it by VPN is not the answer in the long-term. And lastly, they also believe consumers are not being made aware about the type of information the devices are able to collect. (ISACA, ISACA Survey, 2015) In the world of Internet of Things, a vast quantity of data is being collected by devices and the consumers might not even be aware of this fact. This data could be used against them if they are not careful or it could simply be sold on the dark web for sinister purposes.

Consumers have always been sensitive about privacy. Usually, when it comes to privacy, they want more information and increased engagement. It is important to learn about the perception the consumers have regarding privacy, because moving forward with Internet of Things, this we be central to most of the products and systems. And if the consumers have trust issues or do not find the IoT devices secure enough, there could be problems with implementation of the Internet of Things. Every single device and platform in the IoT space might present a potential risk or threat that can be exploited to damage consumers by enabling unauthorized access and misusing the personal information, facilitating attacks on other systems or even by creating hazards to personal safety. (SACMAT, 2016)

With IoT another problem to manage privacy is that there is too much data, according to literature, less than 10,000 homes can create 150 million discrete data points every day. This can create more entry points for hackers and leave delicate information susceptible. (Meola, 2016) Customers may feel violated when the information they share is being used without their knowledge or permission. To have equilibrium between the information that the businesses need while making sure the consumers feel like they are receiving something of value in return. More information should be provided to the customers to make them satisfied and more aware of the entire process.

In a Business Intelligence survey of top technological executives, the concerns of the companies regarding IoT also came to the forefront. Many of the respondents said that privacy and security concerns associated with the Internet of Things is the major barrier in hindering investment. (Weissman, 2015) And if the investment is not flowing that might stop internet of things from reaching its true potential or at least slow down the entire process.

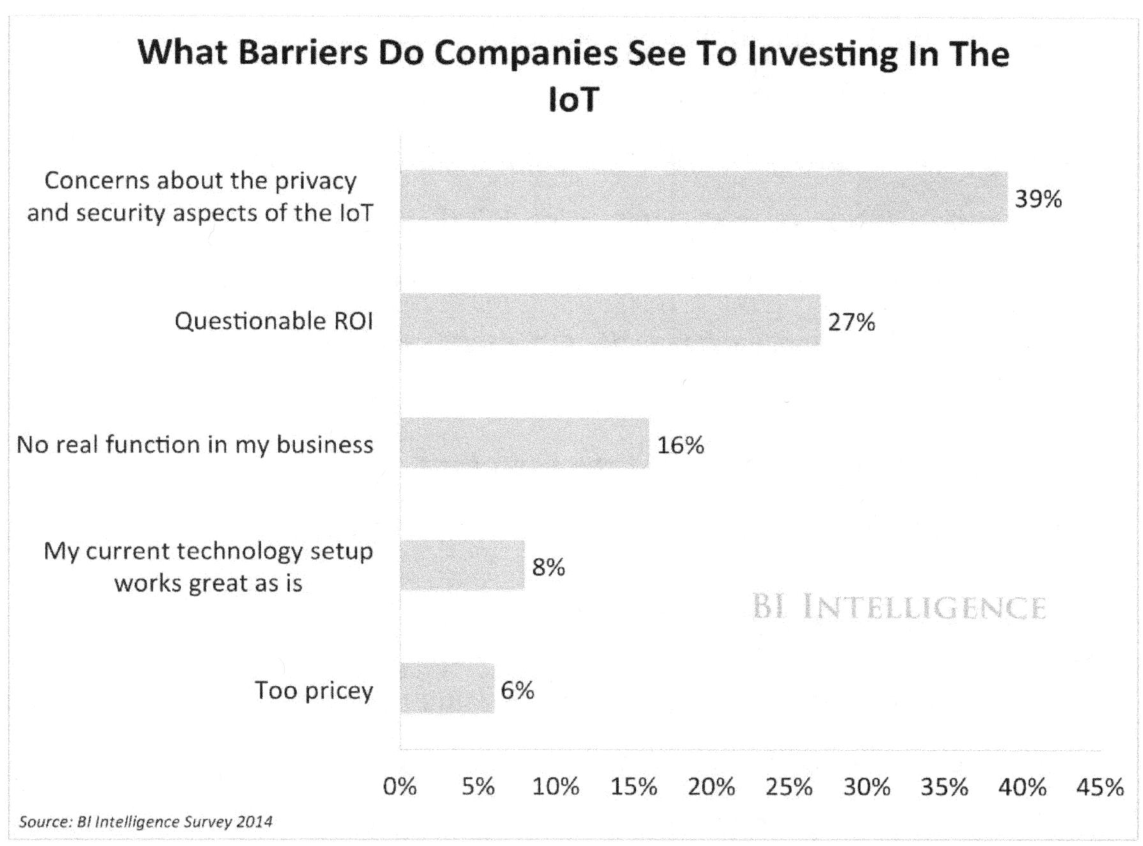

Figure 8 Business Insider Report (Weissman, 2015)

Privacy includes the concealment of personal information as well as the ability to control what happens with this information. The Government and regulatory framework should also play its part when it comes to privacy. "Privacy is documented as a fundamental human right in the 1948 Universal Declaration of Human Rights and is anchored in the constitutional law of most countries today." (Ziegeldorf, Morchon, & Wehrle, Privacy in the Internet of Things: threats, 2013) Unfortunately, now, the extent of privacy protection presented by law is inadequate. As everyday data leaks and unpunished privacy breaches clearly indicate, the IoT will certainly create some grey areas having abundant space to side-step legislative limitations. With the IoT developing fast, legislature side is certain to drop farther behind. Which is why the need for having an adequate legal framework has never been more, this can help the consumers and the industry by increasing trust.

To some up, the underlining problem with Internet of Things and Privacy is the fact that current security measure does not fill the consumers up with confidence and guarantee privacy. While the users with more technical knowledge have a better perception of risks when using IoT devices and applications, majority of the population is still likely to be dumb founded by this talk. The IoT architecture has changed the way we have thought about securing privacy and indeed to have a secure environment, there need to be a combined effort made by the industry and the consumers, because at the end of the day, the stakes are too high to be relaxed. (Weber, 2010)

2.7) Value Perception of Internet of Things

It is very important to understand what Value is. Potentially, all objects could be equipped with sensors and have Internet connectivity. The thing that makes objects "smart" is the capacity to translate and contextualize raw-data in ways that are useful to society.

When it comes to the mass adoption of Internet of Things and the devices it entails, perceived value will be a big deciding factor. How much do consumers value security? It is important to ask question such as; how are they being provided value and how much in monetary terms would they be willing to pay for it? If the value provided by a device or application is what the consumers were searching for, maybe they buy the products regardless of its security vulnerabilities and threats to their privacy. For the industry, it is important to ask questions such as, what do the customers see value in? What segment or type of products are the most sought after? Does increased value mean, people will share more information to get it? Customers may be looking for value, when purchasing products and services, but they also must think about the personal information that they must give out to use those services and products. Almost all IoT devices will use some personal information as a form of input! And on the flip side they should also ask the questions of why certain products or category (home appliances) of products are not value by consumers? Is it because of lack of awareness about them or they are simply not attractive? The industry, to enhance their development process, should also know if the value of a certain product or application is more, will the consumers be willing to give more data to use it and sacrifice their security? Rather than seeing it as a hindrance, there are many opportunities to complete this information value loop with consumers. Internet of Things is creating opportunities for corporations to generate and capture this value in unforeseen places and methods, including connected wearable fitness monitors, insurance policies, pill bottles that know when you've opened them, retail supply chains, and even tennis racquets. Let us take the example of a tennis player, the player does not just value the stiffness of the racquet's frame, the string tension, the weight and balance. He/she might as well learn to value it as a basis of information about the tennis stroke and how it can be improved. In some other industries such as the automotive sector and home insurance, customers have not as much of a say in how corporations use their data. While the flip side of the coin has some businesses such as retail, that are extremely influenced and possibly constrained by their customers' word. Marketers could help the businesses seek a new balance that can create business value along with giving customers at the very least, an insight of choice and value. (Sniderman & Raynor, 2015)

Interestingly, according to the research conducted by Accenture in 2015, most of the people were using an IoT devices for security purposes. (Wilson, Shah, & Whipple, 2015) This situation can be considered somewhat ironic as the people might not know of the security risks associated with the devices themselves. But since 2015, Internet of Things has come a long way, and it would not be a surprise if the result of the finding shows an unfamiliar perspective compared to previous researches. Apart from security, other segments of Internet of Things also show significant economic growth for the future, to judge the familiarity and interest of the consumers in these segments can prove to be valuable insight into their future buying behaviour and let the industry personnel know which segments require priority in terms of enhancing security and protection measures.

What People Really Want from the Internet of Things

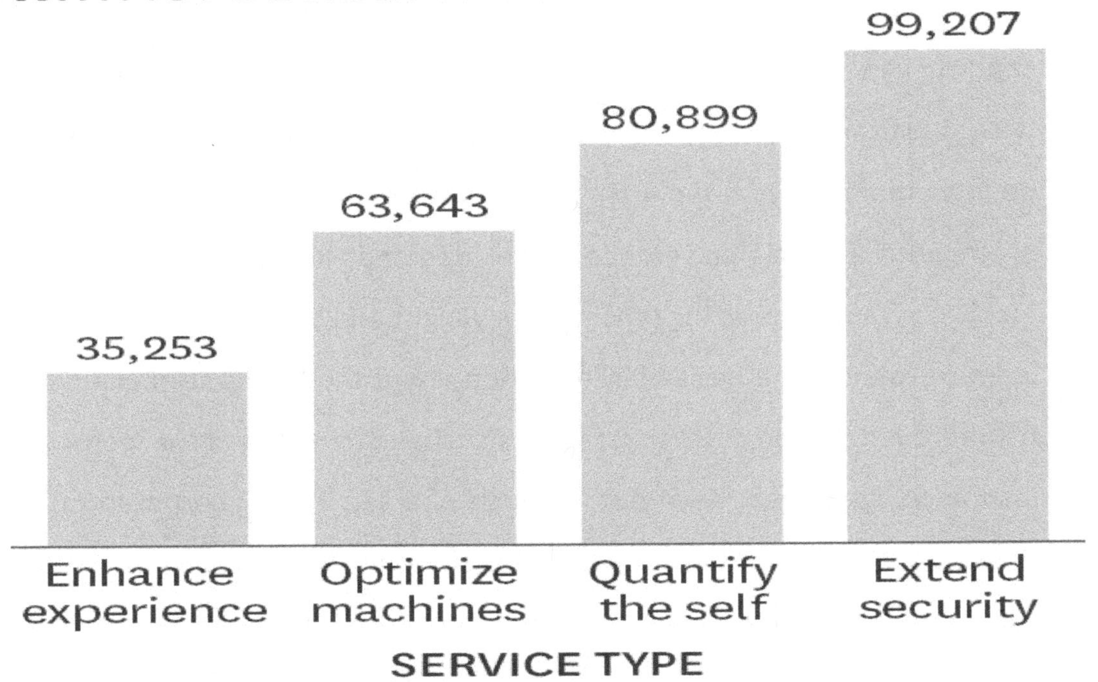

SOURCE ACCENTURE NETWORK ANALYSIS OF 1,000 IOT TECHNOLOGY PLATFORMS AND PLATFORM COMPLEMENTORS, MAY–SEPTEMBER 2015

© HBR.ORG

Figure 9 Value Identification (Wilson, Shah, & Whipple, 2015)

Most of the past research seems to point at both lack of awareness and value perception as the top barriers to mass adoption of this technology among consumers. (Accenture, 2014) It is also important to realize the fact that value perception would be a key element of industry rivalry in the years to come. With the companies who realize it earlier, what it is the consumers see value in and how to show it to them, they will benefit a great deal. A point which was clearly made by many authors in the literature was "Consumers demand value in exchange for their data. Primarily in monetary form, but also in the form of time, energy, and convenience." (Weber, 2010) The author finds it interesting to also study, how much the consumers value security. ISACA's research demonstrated that consumers expected to value businesses that can validate their proficiency in and obligation to cyber securities' best practices. Globally, most of the consumers said it is imperative that security/data specialists possess a cyber security certification if they are working at corporations with access to their customers confidential information (US 89%, Australia 93%, India 96%, Mexico 98%, UK 90%). (ISACA, ISACA Survey, 2015)

What is important for businesses to realize is that if they can capitalize on this opportunity, there is tremendous revenue to be made here. While it is true that mass adoption of connected technology is likely in the long term, research suggests most consumers had not even heard of the term, "The Internet of Things," (Accenture, 2014) The Internet of Things has a lot of potential and is changing the way society functions, but this transition into the new age can be made a lot smoother if the consumers were understood better by the industry. In simple terms, consumers are more willing to share data if offered Value in Return. Businesses can capitalize on revenue opportunities in the IoT space by demonstrating value being created of devices or applications for consumers. The value on offer should be presented in a way that is easily understandable by all types of consumers, be it with or without technical knowledge of Internet of Things.

3) Research Methodology and Research Method

The terms ‘research method’ and ‘research methodology’ are often used interchangeably. However, before getting into the designed methodology and selected methods for this thesis, it is imperative to first clearly define the two terms from literature to develop an enhanced understanding of the whole concept.

Methods are the techniques and procedures implemented to attain and analyse data. This, can include questionnaires, observation and interviews as well as both quantitative (statistical) and qualitative (no statistical) analysis. In contrast, the term **methodology** refers to the theory of how research should be commenced. (Saunders, Lewis, & Thornhill, 2009)

Research is something that people undertake to find out things in a systematic way, in so doing they increase their knowledge. Two important phrases are there in this definition, ‘systematic way’ and ‘to find out things’. Systematic advocates that the research is founded on logical relationships and not only beliefs. To find out things advocates that there is an array of possible purposes for ones’ research. These purposes can be describing, explaining, understanding, analysing and criticising. (Saunders, Lewis, & Thornhill, 2009)

Basic research ←	→ Applied research
Purpose:	*Purpose:*
• Expand knowledge of processes of business and management	• Improve understanding of particular business or management problem
• Results in universal principles relating to the process and its relationship to outcomes	• Results in solution to problem
	• New knowledge limited to problem
• Findings of significance and value to society in general	• Findings of practical relevance and value to manager(s) in organisation(s)
Context:	*Context:*
• Undertaken by people based in universities	• Undertaken by people based in a variety of settings including organisations and universities
• Choice of topic and objectives determined by the researcher	• Objectives negotiated with originator
• Flexible time scales	• Tight time scales

Figure 10 Basic and Applied Research (Saunders, Lewis, & Thornhill, 2009)

3.1) The Research Process

Research is a multi-stage process that one must follow to undertake and complete the research project. Throughout literature, the research process is presented as a series of linked stages and gives the appearance of being organised in a linear manner. For reviewing literature, there are two major reasons, first is the initial search that helps to generate and refine research ideas. Second is often referred to as the **critical review** or **critical literature review**, it is the part of research project. Most research textbooks, will argue that this critical review of literature is essential. (Saunders, Lewis, & Thornhill, 2009)

To build a solid foundation of one's research, it is important and wise to review the literature critically. With the help of literature, it can be easy to find theories/ ideas that can be later tested using data. This is known as a **deductive approach** in which a theoretical or conceptual framework is developed, which is subsequently tested using data. While in some research projects, one plans to explore data to develop theories from it that will afterward relate to the literature. This is known as an **inductive approach**. While the research purpose is still clearly defined with research question(s) and objectives, it does not however start with predetermined theories or conceptual frameworks. (Saunders, Lewis, & Thornhill, 2009)

In summary, to correctly preform the critical literature review section, the following 3 steps need to be completed:

1. Must contain the vital academic theories within the chosen area of research.
2. Must determine that the knowledge of the chosen area is up to date.
3. Must have clear referencing.

Being critical in reviewing the literature is therefore, a combination of skills and the attitude with which the literature is read. It is important to go through the literature about the selected research topic with appropriate cynicism and be eager to question what is being read. (Saunders, Lewis, & Thornhill, 2009)

The deductive approach should be used when a theory is developed along with the hypothesis and then a research strategy to test the respective hypothesis is designed. Whereas the inductive Approach entails collecting data and developing a theory because of the data analysis. (Saunders, Lewis, & Thornhill, 2009) Insofar as it is useful to attach these **research approaches** to the research philosophies, deduction does owe more to positivism and induction to interpretivism. Followers of induction would criticise deduction because of its inclination to construct an inflexible methodology that does not permit alternative explanations of what is going on. In that sense, there is an air of finality about the choice of theory and definition of the hypothesis. While using the inductive approach for conducting research makes the framework in which such proceedings were taking place particularly important. This makes study of a small sample of themes more suitable. It is also possible to combine deduction and induction within the scope of research and in certain cases it is advantageous to do so. (Saunders, Lewis, & Thornhill, 2009)

The **research purpose** most frequently used in the research methods' literature is the classification of exploratory, descriptive and explanatory. An **exploratory study** is valuable in finding out 'what is happening?' to try to find fresh insights, to interrogate and to evaluate phenomena in a new way. It is principally useful when the wish of the researcher is to clarify his/her understanding/idea of a problem like being unsure of the exact nature of the problem. The idea of **descriptive research** is to depict a precise profile of persons, events or situations. This might be extension of or indication to a part of exploratory research. However, mostly it is an extension of a part of **explanatory**. (Saunders, Lewis, & Thornhill, 2009)

3.2) Selected Research Methods and Methodology

The research is of exploratory nature and is a combination of qualitative and quantitative methods. **Mixed methods approach** is the general term for when one uses quantitative and qualitative data collection techniques along with analysis procedures in a research design. For data collection, the author will use both interviews and an online survey.

The **survey** approach is typically associated with deductive method. It is quite a common strategy to undertake and is most often undertaken to find answer for the likes of 'what, where, where, how much and how many' questions. Hence, it inclines to be accepted for exploratory and descriptive research. Surveys are also popular because with them a hefty sum of data may be collected from an ample number of people in a very economical method. Often it is obtained using a questionnaire that is administered to a sample, the data is standardised, allowing for an easy comparison later. In general, the survey is perceived as commanding by people, it is both moderately easy to explain and to understand. (Saunders, Lewis, & Thornhill, 2009)

In the first stage two interviews were conducted with experts on the field of IoT. In the second stage, online survey research was conducted to investigate the consumers of Austria and India, with regards to their awareness of IoT Vulnerabilities, perception towards IoT Privacy and Value. For the second stage, which is the quantitative survey, the demographic independent variables inquired include gender and nationality; the dependent variables include perception of Privacy, awareness of IoT Vulnerabilities and Perception of Value. The two sample sizes drawn out of the country groups contain representative answers from 150 consumers from each country. These consumers target group was selected based on age and the respondents are all under the age of 50.

3.3) Theoretical Framework

For understanding the research method and objects in a glace and developing an overall picture a theoretical framework was created by the author. The framework shows all the variables being used in the research.

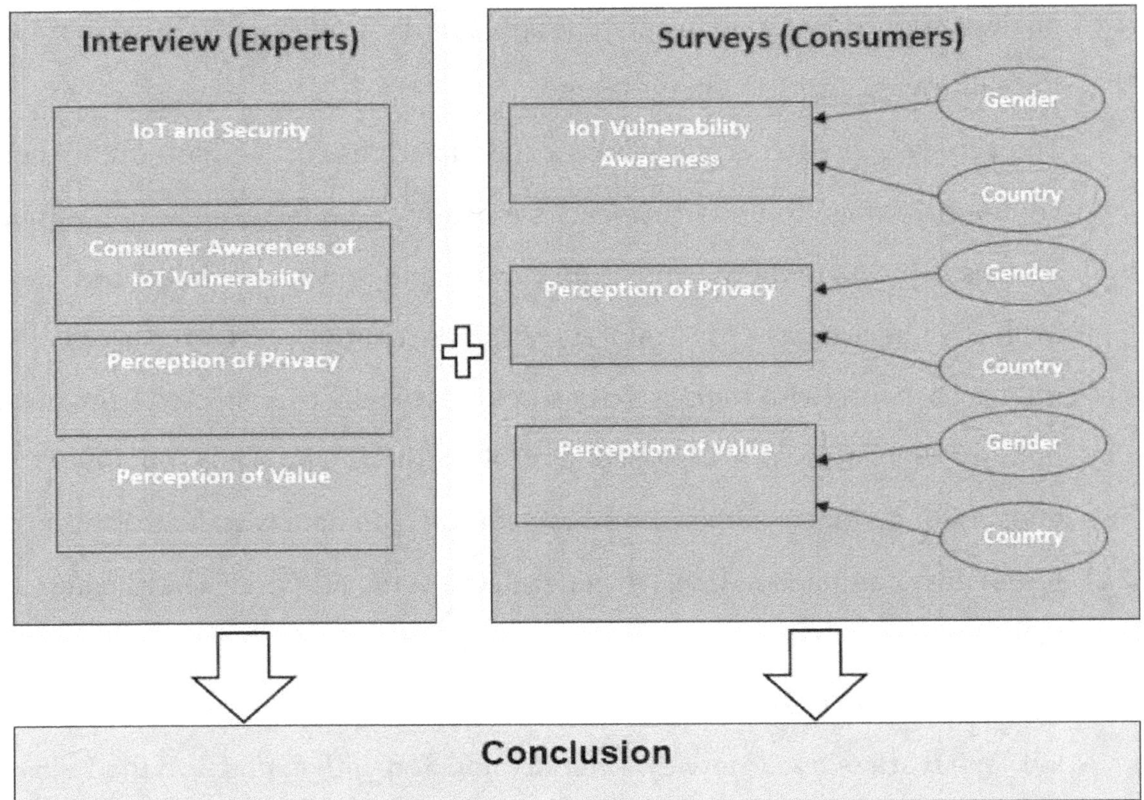

Figure 11 Theoretical Framework

3.4) Research Questions and Variables

Qualitative

RQ: How serious are the security concerns within the realm of IoT technology?

Sub-Questions:

a. Does IoT technology still face security and privacy threats?
b. Do the consumers understand IoT vulnerability? Or this is a gap to be filled?
c. Does cost of IoT products effect the security and privacy?
d. Is the industry playing its part in making secure products and creating consumers aware?
e. What can be done by all the stakeholders to improve security measures within the realm of IoT?

Quantitative

List of Variables:

- Gender (Male and Female)
- Country (Austria and India)
- Consumer Awareness
- Perception of Privacy
- Perception of Value

Hypothesis

After testing the survey, the research questions for the first two sections i.e. Consumer Awareness and Perception of Privacy were divided in to sub questions to be able to test each of them separately. This was an ideal scenario after confirming the Cronbach's Alpha measure. The original plan was to conduct the study with aggregated scores, but at the end it was decided to go for separate tests for the first two sections while the concluding section of Perception of Value will be done with the aggregate method. ***As the questions and hypothesis for the first two sections i.e. Consumer Awareness and Perception of Privacy are very similar, to save time and space the author has only provided the sample (RQA Awareness) of how these would look like. To view the Complete Hypothesis please refer to the Appendix section.***

Awareness

RQ A: How does Gender influence the consumer awareness of the internet of things?

1. I am Familiar with the term Internet of Things.

   H0: Gender does not influence the familiarity with the term Internet of Things.

   H1: Gender does influence the familiarity with the term Internet of Things.

2. How many devices connectable to the internet do I own?

   H0: Gender does not influence the number of connectable devices owned by people.

   H1: Gender does influence the number of connectable devices owned by people.

3. All my devices connectable to the internet are secure.

   H0: Gender does not influence the perceived security of devices connectable to the internet.

   H1: Gender does influence the perceived security of devices connectable to the internet.

4. I regularly update all my devices connectable to the internet.

   H0: Gender does not influence the likely hood of updating devices connectable to the internet.

   H1: Gender does influence the likely hood of updating devices connectable to the internet.

5. More work should be done by the IT industry and the government to educate consumers about internet security.

   H0: Gender does not influence the perception of consumer education with regards to internet security.

   H1: Gender does influence the perception of consumer education with regards to internet security.

RQ B: How does Nationality influence the consumer awareness of the internet of things?

Privacy

RQ A: How does Gender influence the perception of privacy towards the internet of things?

RQ B: How does Nationality influence the perception of privacy towards the internet of things?

Value

RQA: Does being the national of a different country cause a difference in the respondents' value perception with regards to Internet of Things technology?

H0: There is no difference in terms of perceived value with regards to Internet of Things technology between respondents of Austria and India.

H1: There is a difference in terms of perceived value with regards to Internet of Things technology between respondents of Austria and India.

RQB: Does the demographic variable gender cause a difference in respondents' value perception with regards to Internet of Things technology?

H0: There is no difference in terms of perceived value with regards to Internet of Things technology between men and women respondents.

H1: There is a difference in terms of perceived value with regards to Internet of Things technology between men and women respondents.

4) Interview and Survey

4.1) Findings from the Interview

The interviews with the two experts yielded fruitful insights into the world of cyber security and internet of things. Some of the points made by the experts were in line with the literature, however there were certain sections of the interview where they showed a difference of opinion, with the literature and between themselves as well.

Looking at the agreeable points first, both experts said that cyber security is indeed a problem and technologies like the Internet of Things are not completely secure. They believed the progression of Internet of Things has been faster than expected, and they feel it has still not hit its peak popularity. Data security was highlighted as being the most vulnerable, in terms of technological weaknesses. Another point of agreement was the fact that the technological devices available now a day are more in the context of affordability and efficiency which lead the way to giving a less priority to security during the development stage. The basic form of security measures available today for example, having a different password for each connectable device or securing each device separately are highly inconvenient and more works need to be done to come up with better alternatives.

Security techniques are evolving and usually are considered at an early stage in product development. The problem is the fact, to implement those security, can make the products more expensive which would cause the companies to lose markets and profits on the flipside the consumers will also prefer cheaper products.

According to Prof Brickmann the GAP between technology and consumers as increased, they have a lesser understanding of the products they are consuming and that is down to the fact that now the people are more consumption oriented and want to have the latest gadgets without learning more about them. Instead, people should be asking more question and trying to learn more about the products they are using.

However, Prof Marko Bajec had a different opinion on this. He believes that due to the more engaging attitude of consumers towards technology, and increased dependence on technological devices in our daily lives, the GAP has decreased. People understand technology better than they have ever done.

Both agreed that further work should be done by the government to increase awareness about cyber security threats. More laws should be created, there should be stricter industry wide standards. Equal responsibility lies with the industry players and the end consumers to increase awareness about technologies like Internet of Things.

The impact of Internet of Things will only increase in the coming years and this will be a major area of project to the IT sector.

4.2) Survey Questions

After reviewing the previous research form the literature and analysing the interviews, a survey was devised, consisting of 15 questions and split into 3 sections. Each section composed of 5 questions. Now, understandably it was hard to narrow down the 5 questions for each of the topics, as they offer a wide insight into cyber security and the internet of things. The sections for the survey were as follows:

1. Consumer Awareness
2. Perception of Privacy
3. Perception of Value

Consumer Awareness

This section was constructed to test the basic knowledge about the concept of Internet of things and cyber security. In the literature, it was quite clear that previous studies used the term Internet of Things itself to test the populations familiarity, and as a first time for such a research to be done for the Austrian and Indian population, it was decided to carry on with this trend to begin the survey. The second question of the survey address to the basic alertness of the respondents as to him/her at least being aware of the number of connectable devices they own. The third question was devised to check the confidence of the respondents in the security of their connectable devices. In the literature, one of the basic things mentioned as a remedy for security breached was updating the devices regularly, the for the question checked that notion with the respondents to see if the basic measure according to the literature is being met. It was also highlighted by the interviewee that consumer education is a major problem when talking about internet of things and cyber security. The forth question was designed to get the populations take on the matter. All together these 5 questions were deemed enough to gauge the basic awareness of the consumers regarding Internet of Things and Cyber Security.

Perception of Privacy

Cyber security and Privacy has been a well talked about subject and with the emergence of Internet of Things Privacy on the internet has so many areas to be considered however due to time deficiency it was decided to go with the 5 most relevant and least research questions according to literature. The first question is a measure of the basic alertness and counter-measure towards privacy breaches. This question gauges the respondent's readiness towards acting against privacy breaches and alertness to the idea in general as well. The second question highlight how much the privacy is values by respondents, as they answer about their degree of keenness towards not buying technological products due to security and privacy concerns. The third question test if the respondents are considerate and careful while entering personal information or giving it out for using a connectable device. The forth question ask the respondents if they believe hacking and security breaches incidents get enough media coverage. And lastly, the final question of the survey sums up the mood of the respondents with regards to trust in respondents in general as according to the interview, it was suggested that trust could play an important part when it comes to the perception of privacy and the internet of things.

Perception of Value

In the literature, while reviewing the previous research conducted it became very clear that how intrinsic is the perception of value of the consumers to the successful adaptation of the internet of things technology. This section starts off by straight up asking the respondents about their willingness to pay extra to purchase a more secure product. This question is followed by the question in which the respondents are to identify their priorities when purchasing a product that is connectable to the internet. The four aspects (Security, Cost, Feature and Brand) were selected as the main elements of the purchase decision after reviewing the previous research done on the internet of things. The third question vaguely ask the respondents their willingness to give out extra information when it comes to technology. It was decided not to go with a specific type of value offered for this question, as the consumers deferred in what they considered as being "value offered". The following questions deals with the core segments of internet of things and test the respondents interest in the four listed segments. These segments were chosen as they appeared to be the popular ones for the literature. The final question tests the familiarity of the respondents with the four listed segments, to compare if their interest was in any way related to their familiarity with the segments.

5) Results

The number of Women and male respondents were almost the same, which is a good sign for the research. The detailed descriptions of the results can be found in the Appendix section. This section covers the overall results of the survey, without going into the Hypothesis testing.

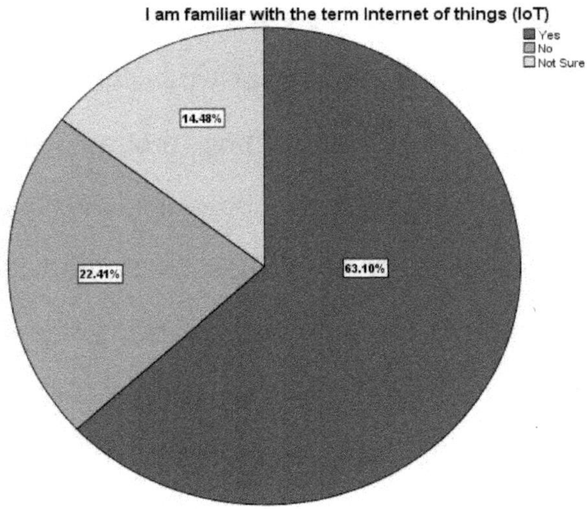

Figure 2 Awareness Q1

An overwhelming majority (63.10 %) of respondents said to be familiar with the term IoT.

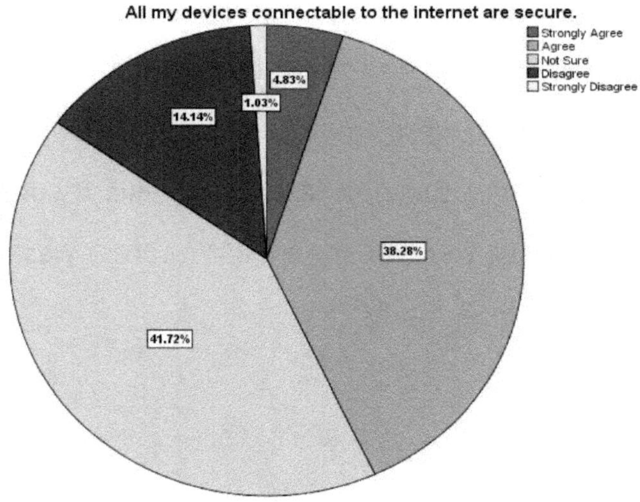

Figure 3 Security

A tiny majority (Agree 38.28% + strongly agree 5%) of people say they are confident about the security of the products they own. 41.72 % said they were not sure about the security of their connectable devices.

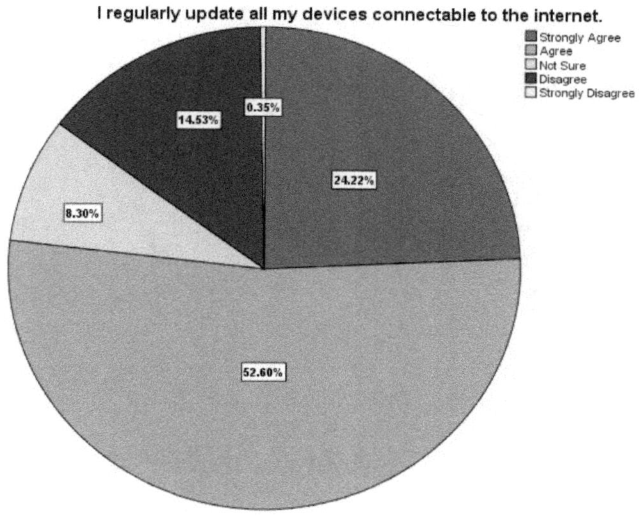

Figure 4 Regular Update

An overwhelming majority said that they regularly update their devices with 24.22% selecting the response Strongly Agree and 52.60% selecting Agree.

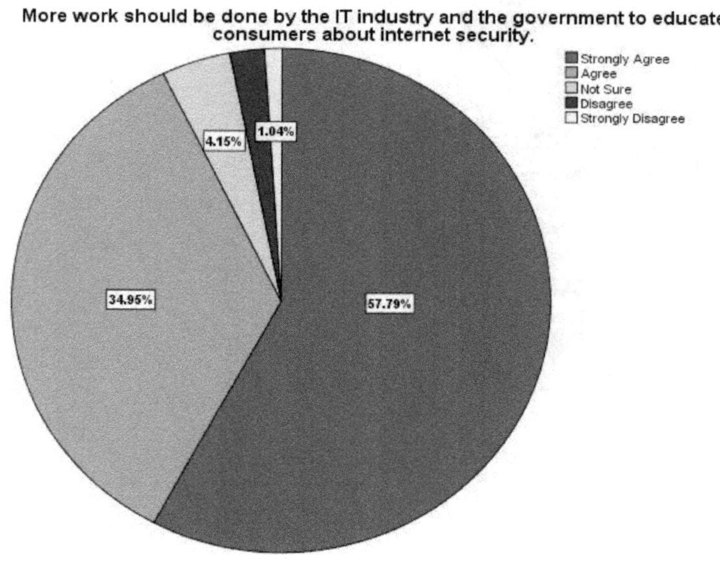

Figure 5 Consumer Education

Majority of respondents said they either Strongly Agreed or Agreed with this statement that more work should be done by the IT industry and the Government to educate consumers about internet security.

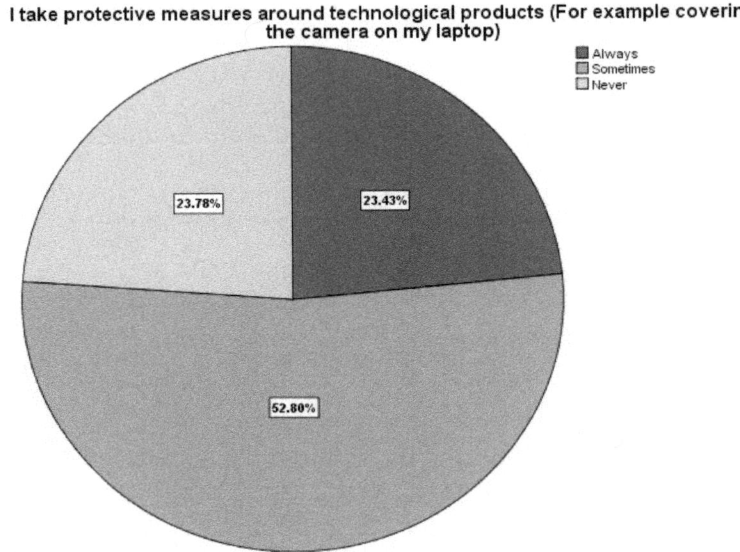

Figure 6 Protective Measure

52.80 % of the people said that they only take protective measures around technology “Sometimes”

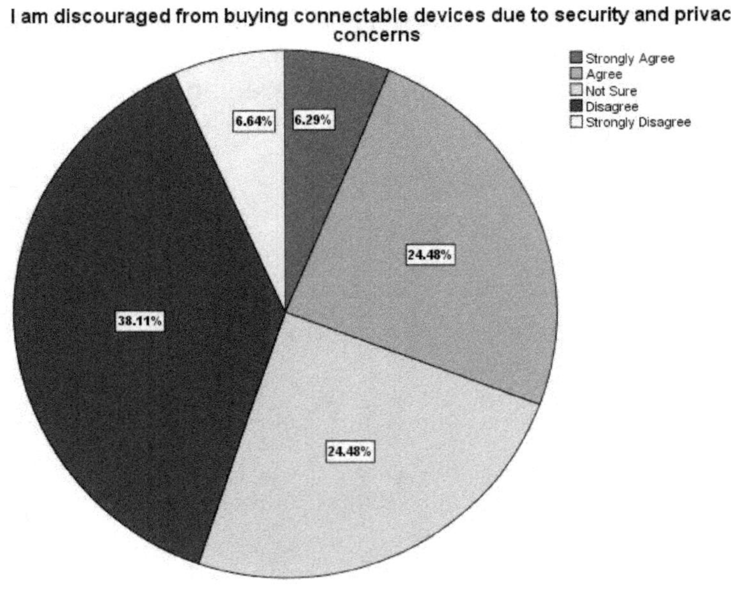

Figure 7 Buying Behaviour

Most people when it comes to buying connectable devices with 38.11% stated that they are not discouraged. 24.48 were Not sure about it while the same amount agreed with the statement.

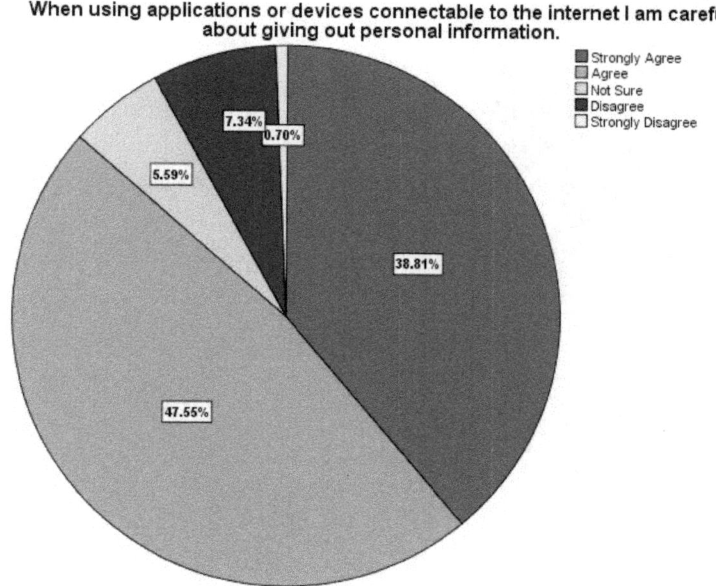

Figure 8 Personal Info

Majority of respondents agree and strongly agree that they are careful while minority state that they are either not sure, disagree with the statement or strongly disagree.

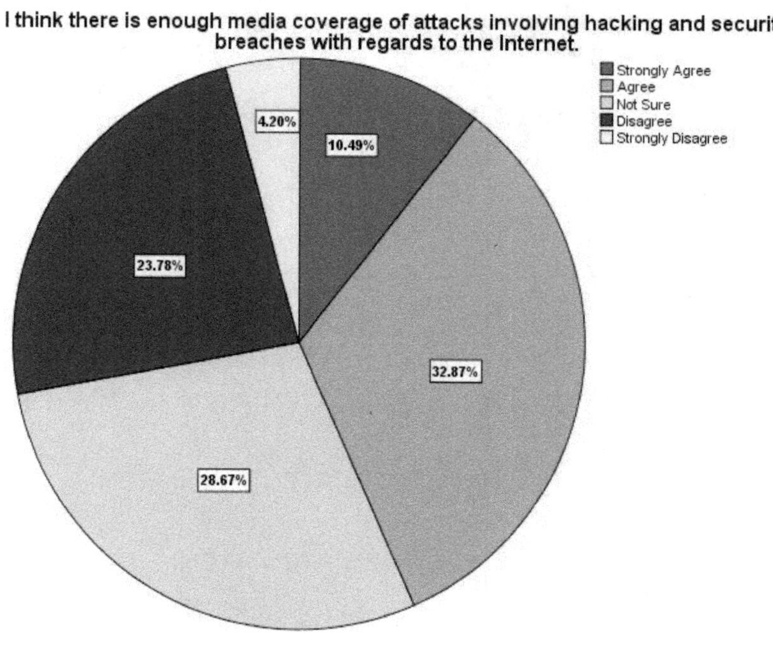

Figure 9 Media Coverage

The respondents showed a diverse feedback on this question, with 32.87 % and 10.49 % agreeing or strongly agreeing respectively with the statement while 23.78 % disagreed and 28.67% were not sure.

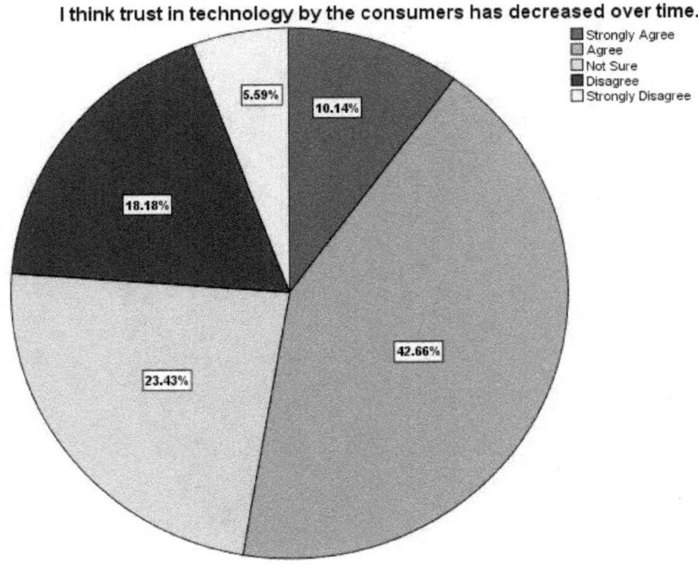

Figure 10 Trust

Most of the respondents agree that the trust in technology has decreased over time.

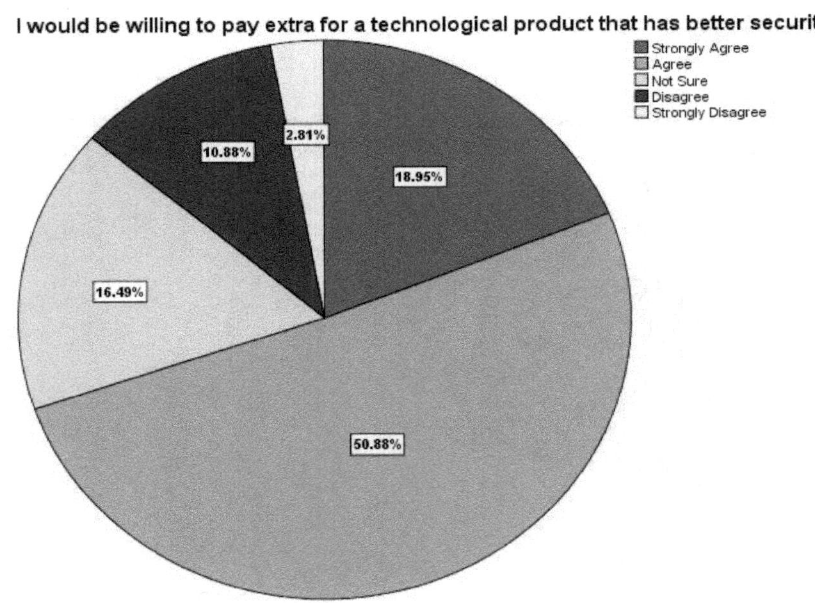

Figure 11 Willingness to Pay

Respondents show that majority would be willing to pay extra in return for better security, which say that security is considered important.

When buying Technological Products, I consider the following elements to be:

	Very Important	Important	Not Sure	Less Important	Not Important
Security	41.20	**42.61**	8.10	7.39	0.70
Cost	38.25	**55.09**	1.05	5.26	0.35
Features	**50.88**	43.26	1.75	3.2	.4
Brand	8.77	34.39	9.82	**36.84**	10.18

Table 1 Buying Technological Products

For most Respondents, Features is a very important factor whereas Security and Cost are Important but interestingly Brand is less important.

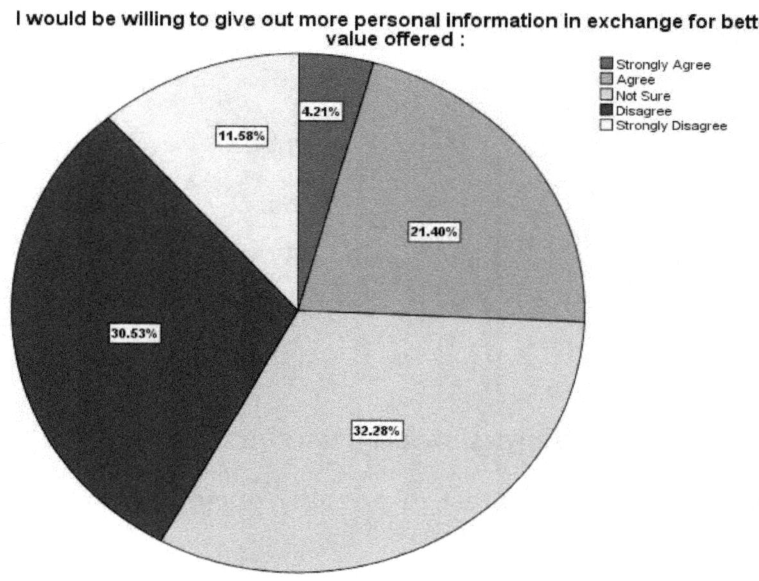

Figure 12 Value Offered vs Personal Info

Most of the people would agree to giving out more personal data in exchange for better value offered.

In terms of buying technological products belonging to the following segments, I would be:

	Very Interested	Interested	Not Sure	Less Interested	Not Interested
Health and Fitness	17.54	**45.26**	9.47	19.65	8.07
Home Appliances	15.79	**44.91**	12.63	20.70	5.96
Home Security	27.11	**38.38**	15.49	13.73	5.28
Automobiles	23.51	**34.74**	9.12	22.11	0.53

Table 2 Products Interest

The respondents show interest in all the segments listed, however the most interest is shown towards Home Security and Health and Fitness.

With regards to technology, I am familiar with the products belonging to the following segments:

	YES	NO
Health and Fitness	**74.04**	25.96
Home Appliances	**66.32**	33.68
Home Security	**57.95**	42.05
Automobiles	**67.84**	32.16

Table 3 Product Familiarity

As most of the respondents showed awareness' towards all the listed segments and showed a likewise interest in possibly buying products belonging to those segments in the future.

5.1) Analysis

In this section, the Hypothesis are tested and the resulting relationships between the variables are portrayed and explained before going into the Discussion Chapter.

While devising the methodology for the analysis of the data collected via surveys, the author decided to use and aggregate score for each section of the survey i.e. Consumer Awareness, Perception of Privacy and Perception of Value. This made sense as all the questions in the survey have equal weight and the process would make analysis efficient and make it easier to interpret the results. However, after using the Cronbach alpha measure to test the survey the first 2 sections of the survey i.e. Consumer Awareness and Perception of Privacy did not show favourable results for an aggregated approach. Consequently, it was decided that for these two sections, the T-Test approach would be better, for which a specific Hypothesis was devised for each question of the survey to better understand the results. The following is an export of the respective Hypothesis that were devised.

I am Familiar with the term Internet of Things.

H0: Gender does not influence the familiarity with the term Internet of Things.

H1: Gender does influence the familiarity with the term Internet of Things.

To save time and make the findings easier to interpret, it was decided to present the summarized results in a table format.

The third section of the survey concerning the Value Perception, did show favourable results in the Cronbach Alpha measure to pursue the aggregated approach.

Cronbach's Alpha for Consumer Awareness:

Reliability Statistics		
Cronbach's Alpha	Cronbach's Alpha Based on Standardized Items	N of Items
.380	.376	3

Table 4 Cronbach Alpha Awareness

Comment: A Cronbach's Alpha of 0.380 suggests that it would be ill advised to aggregate score for the questions belonging to this section of the survey.

Cronbach's Alpha for Perception of Privacy:

Reliability Statistics		
Cronbach's Alpha	Cronbach's Alpha Based on Standardized Items	N of Items
.418	.434	5

Table 5 Cronbach Alpha Privacy

Comment: A Cronbach's Alpha of 0.418 is better than the previous section but it would still be ill advised to aggregate score for the questions belonging to this section of the survey.

Cronbach's Alpha for Perception of Value:

Reliability Statistics		
Cronbach's Alpha	Cronbach's Alpha Based on Standardized Items	N of Items
.708	.700	14

Table 6 Cronbach Alpha Value

Comment: A Cronbach's Alpha of 0.708 is favourable and allows to aggregate score for the questions belonging to this section of the survey.

Consumer Awareness

RQ A: How does Gender influence the consumer awareness of the internet of things?

Summarized Result	Sig.
I am Familiar with the term Internet of Things.	
H1: Gender does influence the familiarity with the term Internet of Things.	.001
How many devices connectable to the internet do I own?	
H1: Gender does influence the number of connectable devices owned by people	.000
All my devices connectable to the internet are secure.	
H1: Gender does influence the perceived security of devices connectable to the internet.	.237
I regularly update all my devices connectable to the internet.	
H1: Gender does influence the likely hood of updating devices connectable to the internet.	.000
More work should be done by the IT industry and the government to educate consumers about internet security.	
H1: Gender does influence the perception of consumer education with regards to internet security.	.032

Table 7 Awareness and Gender Result

The table above shows the result for consumer awareness section with regards to the variable gender. The H1 is accepted overall (3/5) suggesting that Gender does influence the consumer awareness regarding Interent of things.

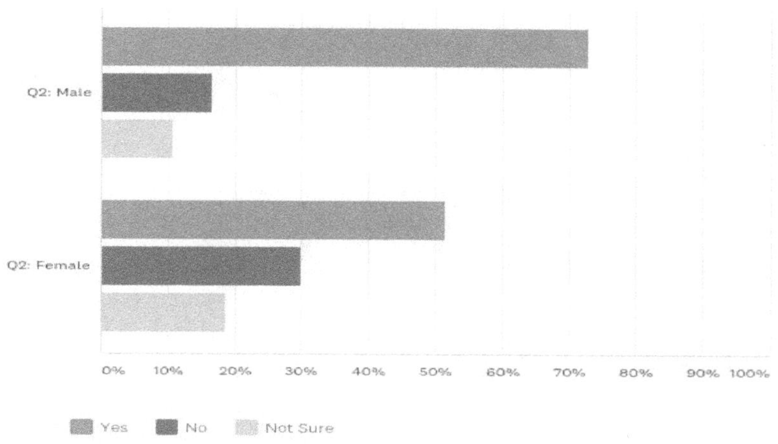

Figure 13 Familiarity Gender

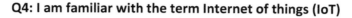

The result of the survey indicates that although there has been an increase in overall consumer awareness about the internet of things and cyber security, a difference in Gender awareness is prevalent. In all, Men (73%) appear to be more aware compared to Women (51%).

Q5: How many devices connectable to the internet do I own?

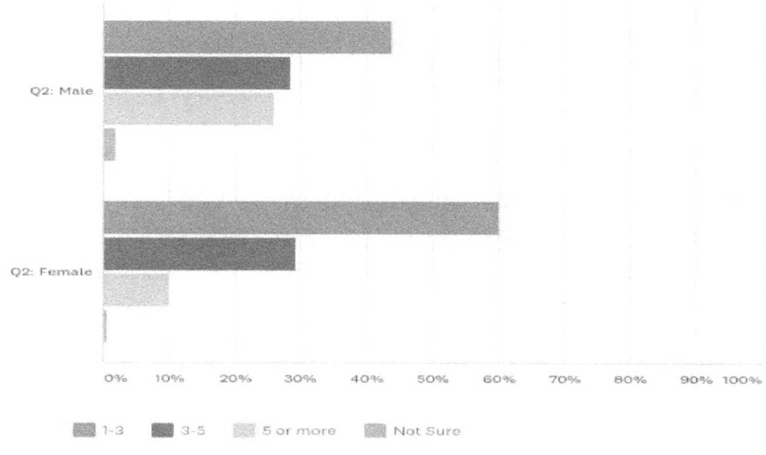

Figure 14 Devices Owned Gender

The Men also tend to own more connectable devices then Women. Or perhaps they are more aware about the devices they.

Q6: All my devices connectable to the internet are secure.

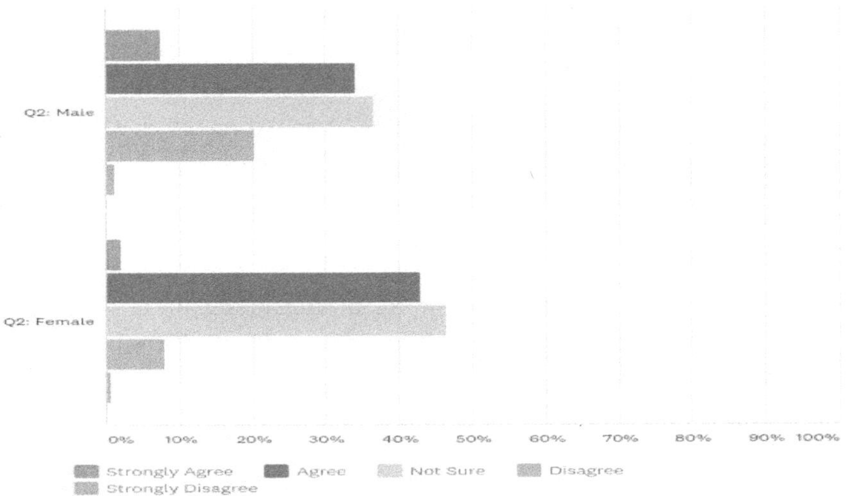

Figure 15 Secure Gender

47% Women are not confident about the security of their connectable devices, with “Not Sure” being the most popular answer. Men 43% majority, are more confident with a combination of “Agree” and “Strongly Agree” responses.

Q7: I regularly update all my devices connectable to the internet.

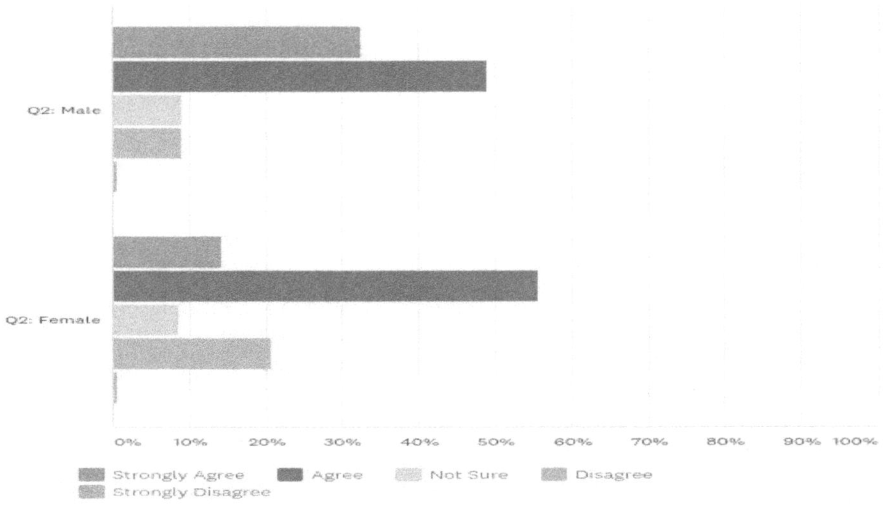

Figure 16 Update Gender

Men are also more likely to regularly update their devices as compared to Women. However, both said they do regularly update.

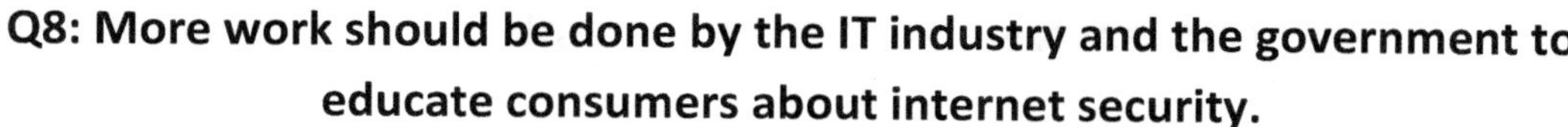

Q8: More work should be done by the IT industry and the government to educate consumers about internet security.

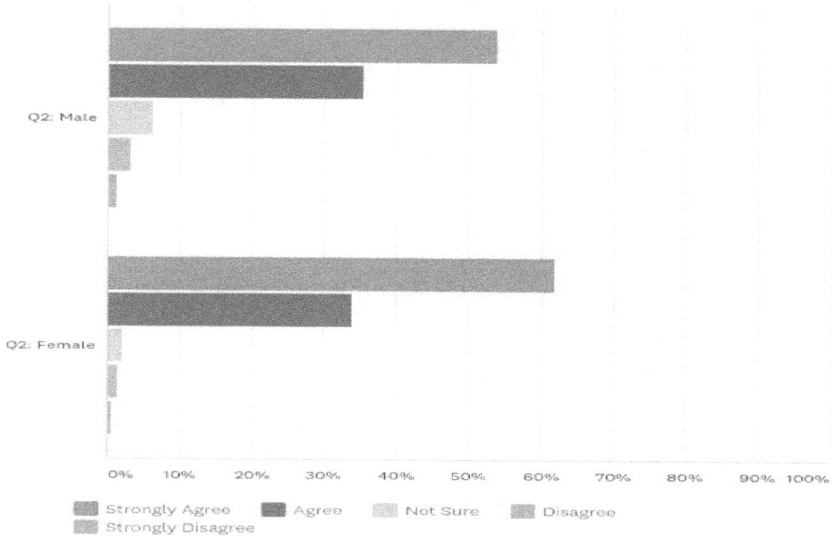

Figure 17 Education Gender

Both genders overwhelmingly agree to the fact that more work needs to be done to educate consumers about the vulnerabilities of the Internet of Things.

RQ B: How does Nationality influence the consumer awareness of the internet of things?

Summarized Result	Sig.
I am Familiar with the term Internet of Things.	
H1: Nationality does influence the familiarity with the term Internet of Things.	.974
How many devices connectable to the internet do I own?	
H1: Nationality does influence the number of connectable devices owned by people	.104
All my devices connectable to the internet are secure.	
H1: Nationality does influence the perceived security of devices connectable to the internet.	.063
I regularly update all my devices connectable to the internet.	
H1: Nationality does influence the likely hood of updating devices connectable to the internet.	.231
More work should be done by the IT industry and the government to educate consumers about internet security.	
H1: Nationality does influence the perception of consumer education with regards to internet security.	.010

Table 8 Awareness and Nationality Result

The table above shows the consumer awareness section with regards to the variable nationality. The H1 is rejected in all the questions, suggesting that there is no influence of nationality when it comes to consumer awareness regarding Internet of Things.

Q4: I am familiar with the term Internet of things (IoT)

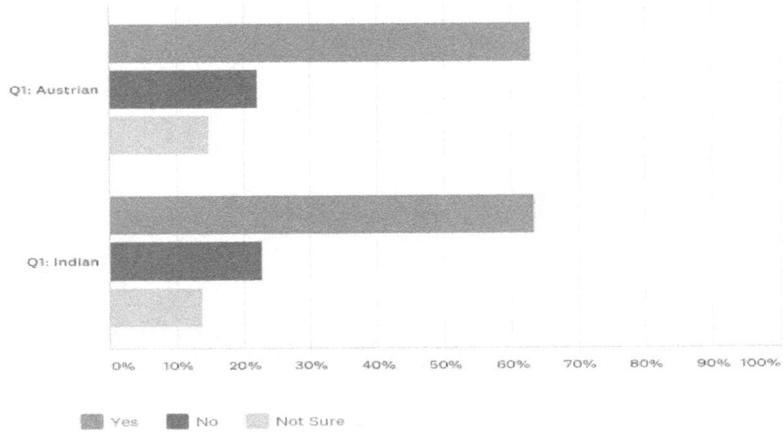

Figure 18 Familiarity Nationality

In terms of the influence of Nationality, the results of the survey show it does not influence consumer awareness. Moreover, respondents of both countries had similar thoughts, there was an increased awareness overall.

Q5: How many devices connectable to the internet do I own?

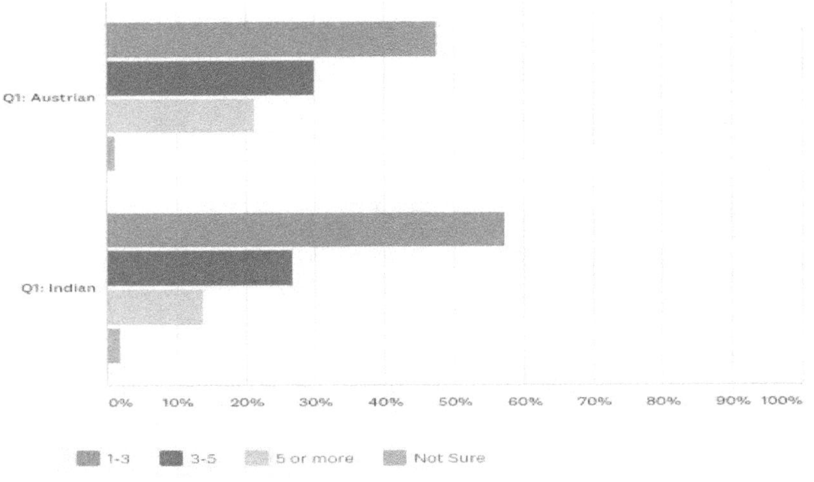

Figure 19 Devices owned Nationality

Connectable devices owned by the respondents from the two countries also show equivalent results with the majority (51%) stating that they own between 1-3.

Q6: All my devices connectable to the internet are secure.

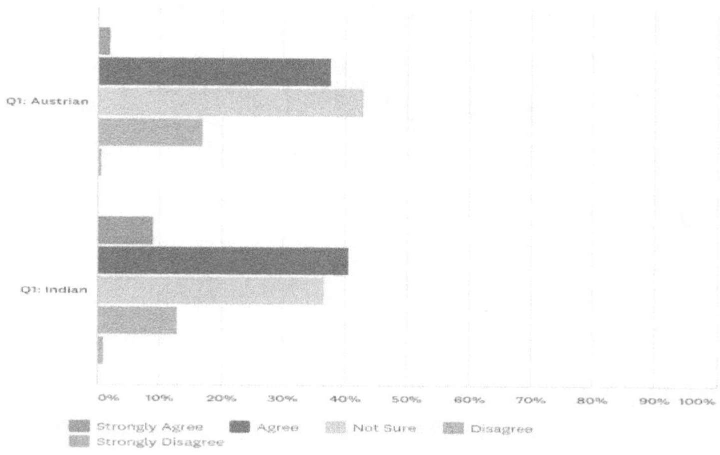

Figure 20 Security Nationality

Most Austrian (43%) said they were "Not Sure" if all their devices connectable to the internet were secure. However, a slight majority (49%) more of the Indian said that they would "agree" or "strongly agree" with this statement.

Q7: I regularly update all my devices connectable to the internet.

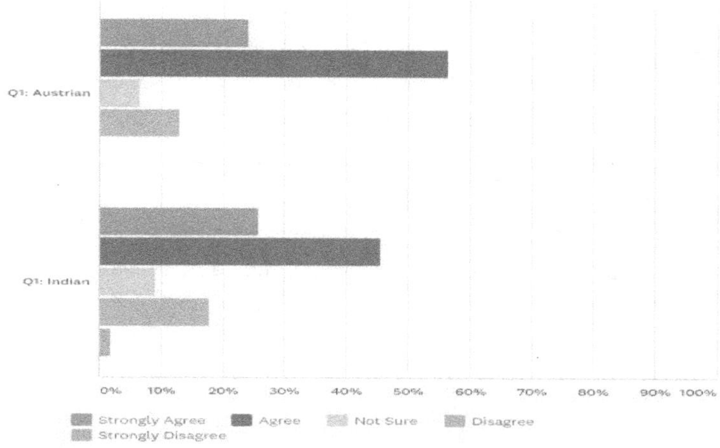

Figure 21 Updates Nationality

For this question, results were similar from the two countries, respondents from both (81% Austrians, 71% Indians) said that they do regularly update their connectable devices.

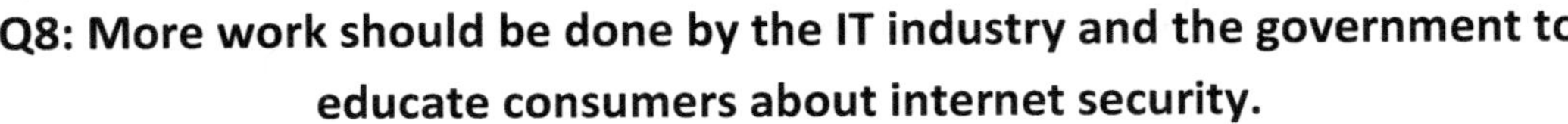

Q8: More work should be done by the IT industry and the government to educate consumers about internet security.

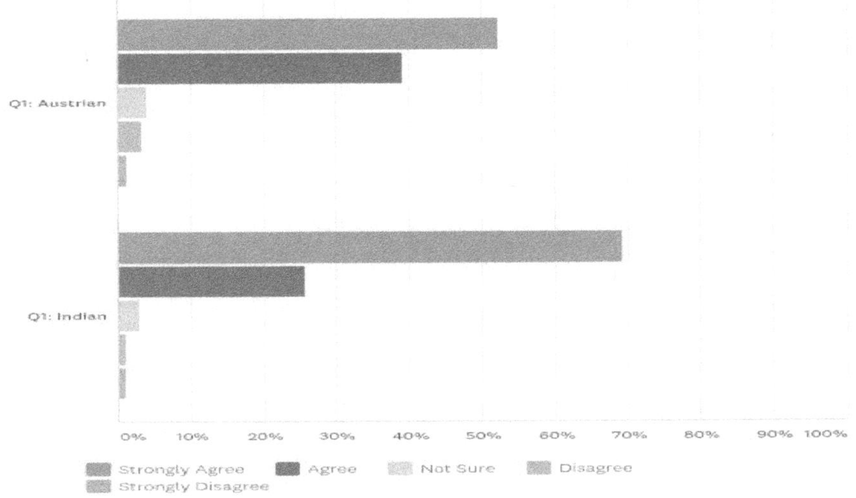

Figure 22 Education Nationality

Respondents overwhelmingly agreed with the statement, suggesting that they do believe a lot more needs to be done to bridge the gap.

Perception of Privacy

RQ A: How does Gender influence the perception of privacy towards the internet of things?

Summarized Result	Sig.
I take protective measures around technological products (For example covering the camera on my laptop)	
H1: Gender does influence protective behaviour around technological products.	*.672*
I am discouraged from buying connectable devices due to security and privacy concerns	
H1: Gender does influence the tendency to buy connectable devices due to security and privacy concerns	*.173*
When using applications or devices connectable to the internet I am careful about giving out personal information.	
H1: Gender does influence the tendency to give out personal information on connectable devices.	*.685*
I think there is enough media coverage of attacks involving hacking and security breaches with regards to the Internet.	
H1: Gender does influence perception about media coverage of attacks involving hacking and security breaches with regards to the Internet.	*.310*
I think trust in technology by the consumers has decreased over time.	
H1: Nationality does influence the perception of consumer education with regards to internet security.	*.007*

Table 9 Privacy and Gender Result

The table above gives the summary of the T-Test Analysis for the Perception of Privacy section with regards to the variable Gender. All the questions had h1 was rejected, suggesting that Gender does not have an influence when it comes to the Perception of privacy for the population.

Q9: I take protective measures around technological products (For example covering the camera on my laptop)

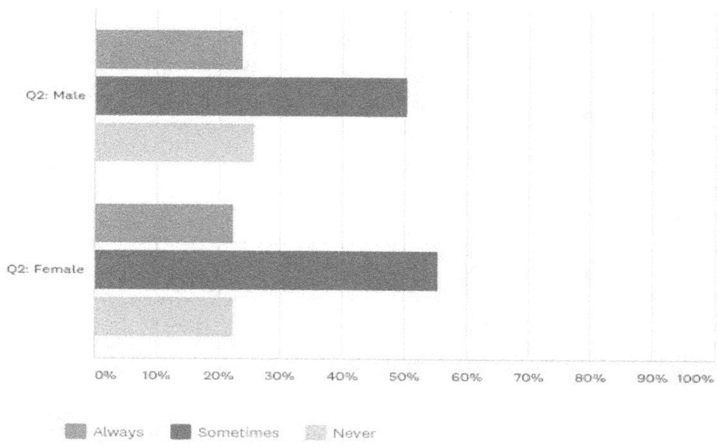

Figure 23 Protective Measures Gender

The results show that Gender has no influence on the perception of privacy. Privacy gets treated in an equivalent way by men and women, both said in majority that they only sometimes take protective measures around technological products connected with the internet.

Q10: I am discouraged from buying connectable devices due to security and privacy concerns

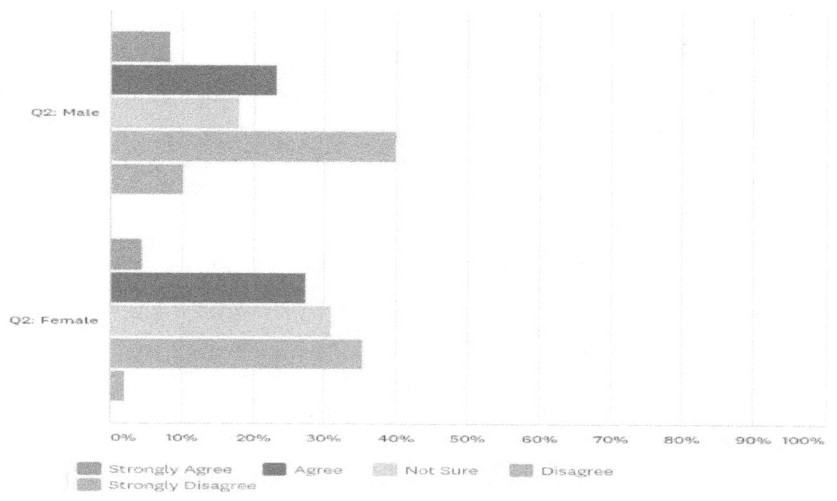

Figure 24 Buying Behaviour Gender

Also, privacy and security concerns put off neither men (51%) or women (57 %) from buying products. The buying interests is not fazed by the concerns in most cases.

Q11: When using applications or devices connectable to the internet I am careful about giving out personal information.

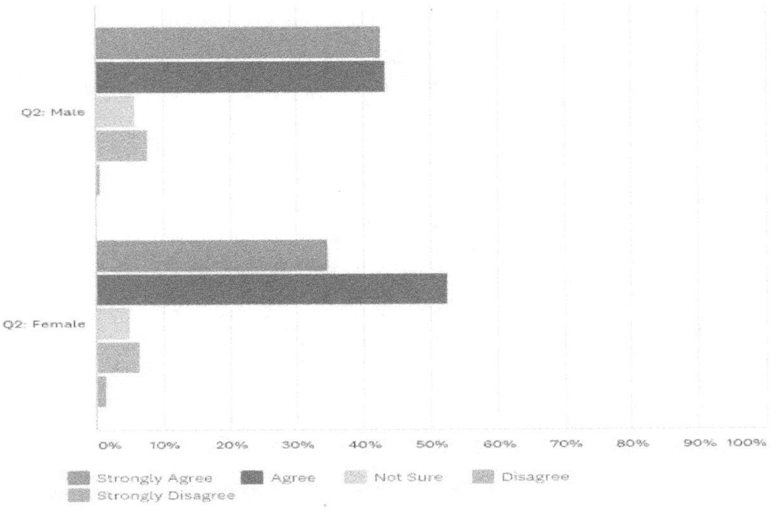

Figure 25 Personal Info Gender

Both Genders (86%men, 87% women) said that they are careful about giving out personal information when using devices or applications connected to the internet

Q12: I think there is enough media coverage of attacks involving hacking and security breaches with regards to the Internet.

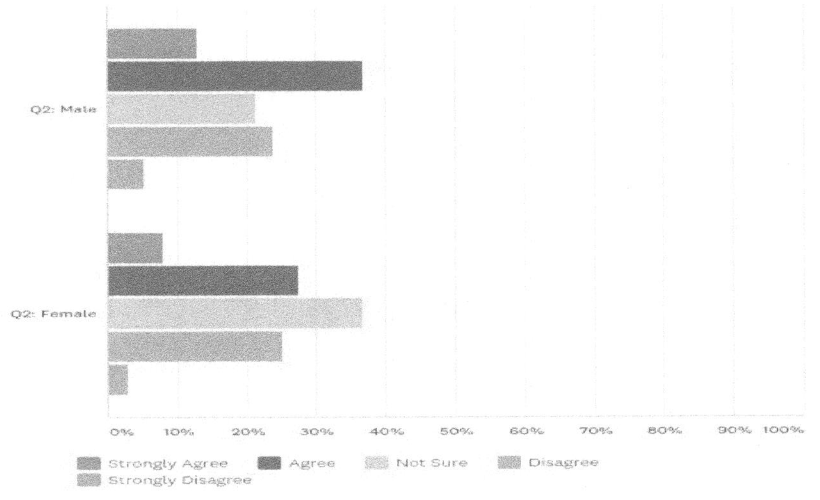

Figure 26 Media Coverage Gender

There does seems to be a slight difference between how both genders perceive media coverage surrounding hacking and security breaches. Most of the men (49%) said it's enough coverage while majority of the women (37%) were "Not Sure" about it.

Q13: I think trust in technology by the consumers has decreased over time.

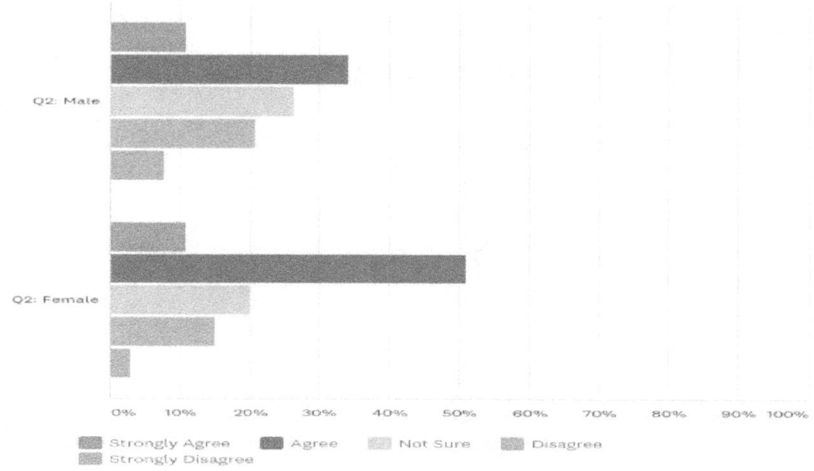

Figure 27 Trust Gender

Lastly, both genders (45% men, 62% women) do heavily agree on the statement that trust in technology has decreased over time.

RQ B: How does Nationality influence the perception of privacy towards the internet of things?

Summarized Result	Sig.
I take protective measures around technological products (For example covering the camera on my laptop)	
H1: Nationality does influence protective behaviour around technological products.	*.017*
I am discouraged from buying connectable devices due to security and privacy concerns	
H1: Nationality does influence the tendency to buy connectable devices due to security and privacy concerns	*.015*
When using applications or devices connectable to the internet I am careful about giving out personal information.	
H1: Nationality does influence the tendency to givie out personal information on connectable devices.	*.704*
I think there is enough media coverage of attacks involving hacking and security breaches with regards to the Internet.	
H1: Nationality does influence perception about media coverage of attacks involving hacking and security breaches with regards to the Internet.	*.391*
I think trust in technology by the consumers has decreased over time.	
H1: Nationality does influence the level of trust in technology by the consumers had over time.	*.215*

Table 10 Privacy and Nationality Result

The table above gives the summary of the T-Test Analysis for the Perception of Privacy section with regards to the variable Nationality. In all the questions h1 was rejected, suggesting that Nationality does not have an influence when it comes to the Perception of privacy for the population.

Q9: I take protective measures around technological products (For example covering the camera on my laptop)

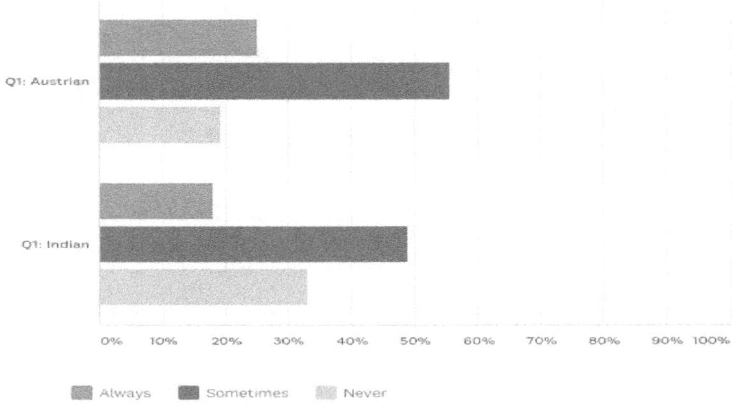

Figure 28 Protective measure Nationality

The results from the two countries show similar trends suggesting that majority (56% Austrians, 49% Indians) only “sometimes” takes protective measures when using connectable devices.

Q10: I am discouraged from buying connectable devices due to security and privacy concerns

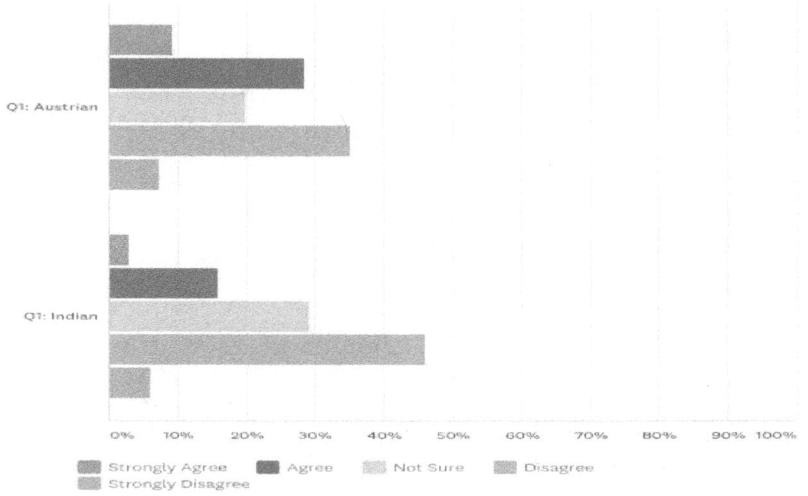

Figure 29 Buying Behaviour Nationality

Indian (52%) respondents said that they are not discouraged from buying due to security and privacy concerns most Austrian (42%) respondents said the same.

Q11: When using applications or devices connectable to the internet I am careful about giving out personal information.

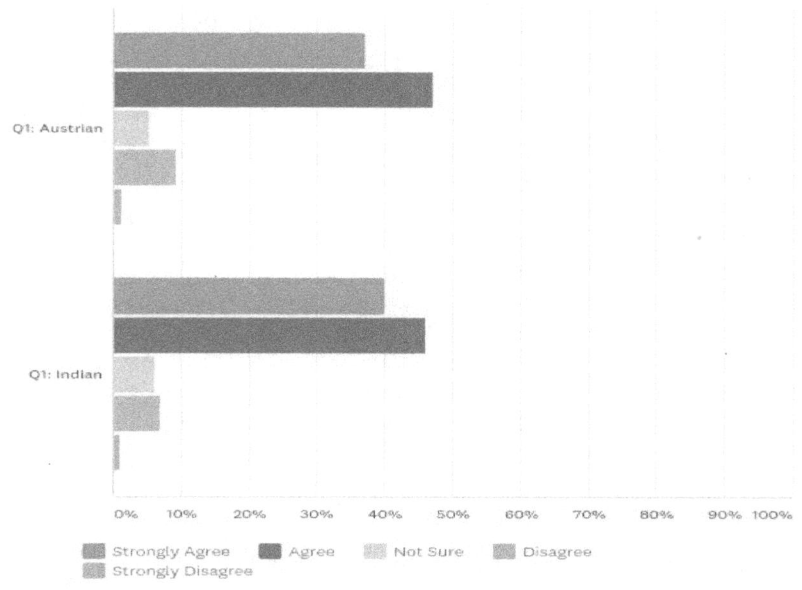

Figure 30 Personal Information Nationality

Interestingly, respondents (86%) from both countries overwhelmingly said that they are careful about giving out personal information when using applications or devices connectable to the internet.

Q12: I think there is enough media coverage of attacks involving hacking and security breaches with regards to the Internet.

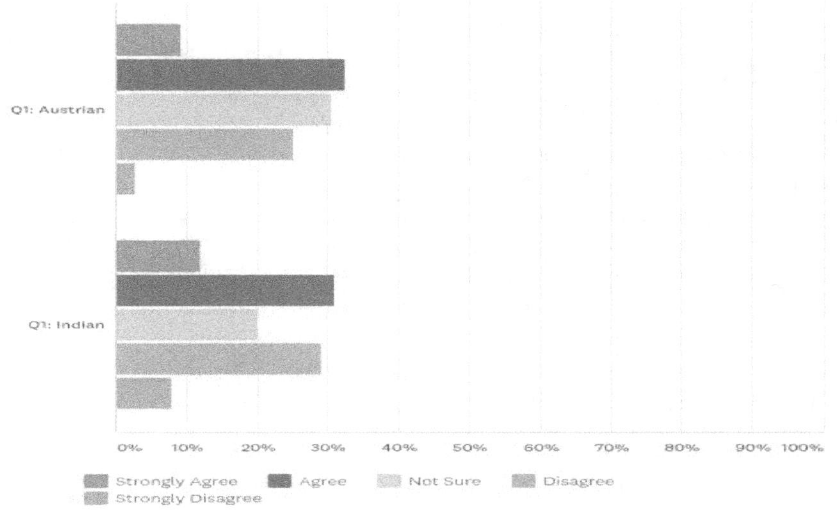

Figure 31 Media Coverage Nationality

Respondents form both countries in majority said that there is enough media coverage of attacks involving hacking and security breaches with regards to the internet.

Q13: I think trust in technology by the consumers has decreased over time.

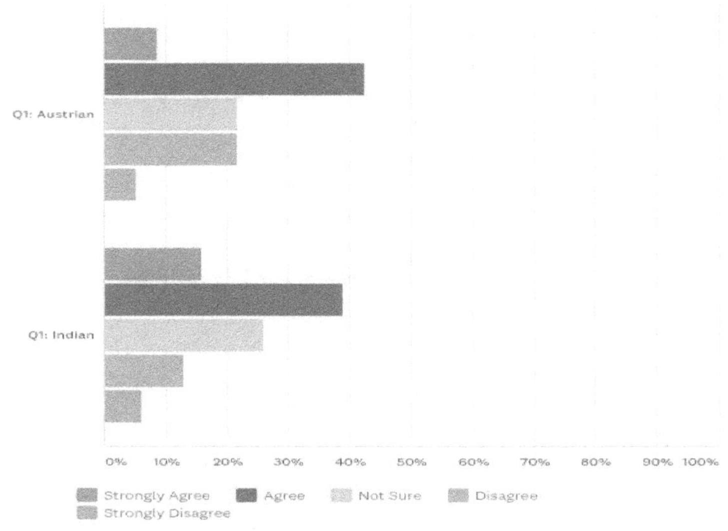

Figure 32 Trust Nationality

Majority (53%) of respondents from both countries “strongly agree” or “agree” with this statement.

Value Perception

RQA: Does being the national of a different country cause a difference in the respondents’ value perception with regards to Internet of Things technology?

Independent Samples Test				
		t-test for Equality of Means		
		df	Sig. (2-tailed)	Mean Difference
Value Perception	Equal variances assumed	241	.000	.43548
	Equal variances not assumed	194.523	.000	.43548

Table 11 Value and Nationality

Summarized Result	Sig.
H1: There is a difference in terms of perceived value with regards to Internet of Things technology between respondents of Austria and India.	.000

Table 12 Value and Nationality Result

The result of the Independent T-test confirms that there is a significant difference in the value perception of respondents depending on the nationality. Which means that the H1 can be accepted.

Q14: I would be willing to pay extra for a technological product that has better security

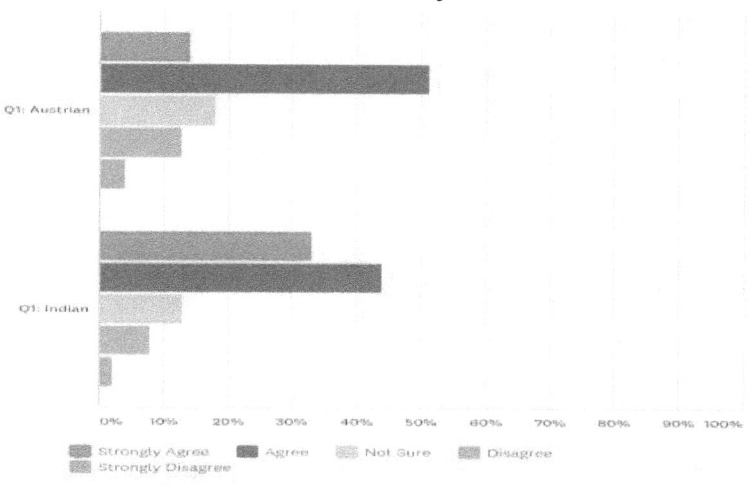

Figure 33 Paying Extra Nationality

Both Nationalities Indian (77%) and Austrian (65%) overwhelmingly said they would be willing to pay extra for a technological product that has better security.

Q15: When buying technological product, I consider the following elements to be:

	VERY IMPORTANT	IMPORTANT	NOT SURE	LESS IMPORTANT	NOT IMPORTANT	TOTAL	WEIGHTED AVERAGE
Security							
Q1: Austrian (A)	32.00% 48 B	49.33% 74 B	10.67% 16	8.00% 12	0.00% 0	60.00% 150	1.95
Q1: Indian (B)	61.62% 61 A	26.26% 26 A	4.04% 4	6.06% 6	2.02% 2	39.60% 99	1.61
Cost							
Q1: Austrian (A)	37.33% 56	56.00% 84	1.33% 2	5.33% 8	0.00% 0	60.00% 150	1.75
Q1: Indian (B)	36.00% 36	56.00% 56	1.00% 1	6.00% 6	1.00% 1	40.00% 100	1.80
Features							
Q1: Austrian (A)	44.00% 66 B	48.67% 73 B	2.00% 3	5.33% 8 B	0.00% 0	60.00% 150	1.69
Q1: Indian (B)	66.00% 66 A	33.00% 33 A	0.00% 0	0.00% 0 A	1.00% 1	40.00% 100	1.37
Brand							
Q1: Austrian (A)	2.67% 4 B	20.00% 30 B	10.67% 16	50.67% 76 B	16.00% 24 B	60.00% 150	3.57
Q1: Indian (B)	19.00% 19 A	52.00% 52 A	9.00% 9	18.00% 18 A	2.00% 2 A	40.00% 100	2.32

Table 13 Elements Nationality

For Indian respondents Features are "very Important", for Austrian they are only "Important". "Cost" is important for both. Brand is "less important" for Austrians, while it is "Important" for Indians.

Q16: I would be willing to give out more personal information in exchange for better value offered:

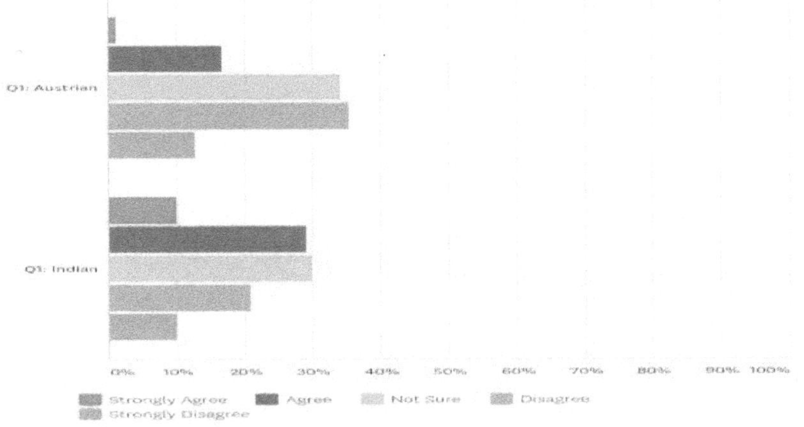

Figure 34 Personal Info Nationality

Surprisingly, 39% Indian respondents showed they would be willing to give out more personal information in exchange for better value offered. Whereas most Austrian 48% would Disagree (Disagree + Strongly Disagree).

Q17: In terms of buying technological products belonging to the following segments, I would be:

	VERY INTERESTED	INTERESTED	NOT SURE	LESS INTERESTED	NOT INTERESTED	TOTAL	WEIGHTED AVERAGE
Health and Fitness							
Q1: Austrian (A)	17.33% 26	34.00% 51 B	10.67% 16	29.33% 44 B	8.67% 13	60.00% 150	2.78
Q1: Indian (B)	19.19% 19	57.58% 57 A	10.10% 10	6.06% 6 A	7.07% 7	39.60% 99	2.24
Home Appliances							
Q1: Austrian (A)	12.00% 18 B	37.33% 56 B	16.00% 24	26.67% 40 B	8.00% 12	60.00% 150	2.81
Q1: Indian (B)	23.00% 23 A	52.00% 52 A	8.00% 8	12.00% 12 A	5.00% 5	40.00% 100	2.24
Home Security							
Q1: Austrian (A)	21.33% 32 B	40.67% 61	13.33% 20	18.00% 27 B	6.67% 10	60.00% 150	2.48
Q1: Indian (B)	42.42% 42 A	36.36% 36	10.10% 10	6.06% 6 A	5.05% 5	39.60% 99	1.95
Automobiles							
Q1: Austrian (A)	11.33% 17 B	28.67% 43	10.67% 16	33.33% 50 B	16.00% 24 B	60.00% 150	3.14
Q1: Indian (B)	48.48% 48 A	39.39% 39	4.04% 4	4.04% 4 A	4.04% 4 A	39.60% 99	1.76

Table 14 Interests Nationality

Both Indians and Austrian are buying interested in Health and Fitness however Indians seems to be more eager. Most Indian interested in Home Appliances compared to a tiny Austrian majority who is interested as well. Both are interested in Home Security and lastly, Austrians show less interest in Automobiles compared to Indian.

Q18: With regards to technology, I am familiar with products belonging to the following segments:

Health and Fitness				
	YES	NO	TOTAL	WEIGHTED AVERAGE
Q1: Austrian (A)	72.67% 109	27.33% 41	60.00% 150	1.27
Q1: Indian (B)	75.00% 75	25.00% 25	40.00% 100	1.25
Home Appliances				
	YES	NO	TOTAL	WEIGHTED AVERAGE
Q1: Austrian (A)	63.33% 95	36.67% 55	60.00% 150	1.37
Q1: Indian (B)	73.74% 73	26.26% 26	39.60% 99	1.26
Home Security				
	YES	NO	TOTAL	WEIGHTED AVERAGE
Q1: Austrian (A)	55.70% 83	44.30% 66	59.60% 149	1.44
Q1: Indian (B)	67.68% 67	32.32% 32	39.60% 99	1.32
Automobiles				
	YES	NO	TOTAL	WEIGHTED AVERAGE
Q1: Austrian (A)	60.14% 89 B	39.86% 59 B	59.20% 148	1.40
Q1: Indian (B)	85.86% 85 A	14.14% 14 A	39.60% 99	1.14

Table 15 Familiarity - Nationality

Majority respondents from both nationalities are familiar with all the listed Segments. Austrian are most Familiar with Health and Fitness while Indian are most Familiar with Automobiles.

RQB: Does the demographic variable gender cause a difference in respondents' value perception with regards to Internet of Things technology?

Independent Samples Test				
		t-test for Equality of Means		
		df	Sig. (2-tailed)	Mean Difference
Value Perception	Equal variances assumed	283	.002	-.15700
	Equal variances not assumed	273.153	.002	-.15700

Table 16 Value and Gender

Summarized Result	Sig.
H1: There is a difference in terms of perceived value with regards to Internet of Things technology between men and women respondents.	.002

Table 17 Value and Gender Result

The result of the Independent T-test confirms that there is a significant difference in the value perception of respondents depending on the gender. Which means that the H1 can be accepted.

Q14: I would be willing to pay extra for a technological product that has better security

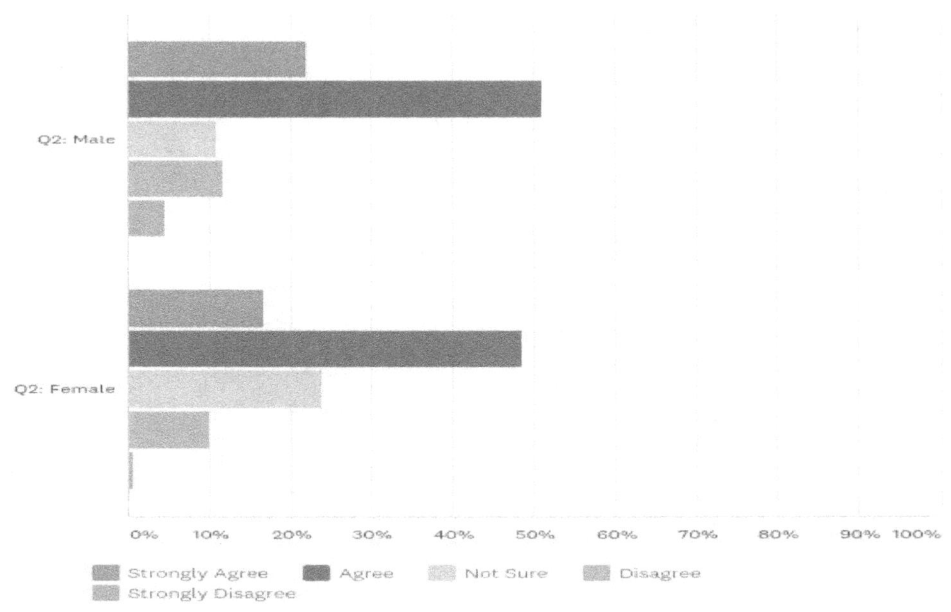

Figure 35 Paying Extra Gender

Majority of men (73%) and women (65%) respondents said they would be willing to pay extra for a product that has better security. Which is also contrary to the literature and to what was said by the experts.

Q15: When buying technological product, I consider the following elements to be:

	VERY IMPORTANT	IMPORTANT	NOT SURE	LESS IMPORTANT	NOT IMPORTANT	TOTAL	WEIGHTED AVERAGE
Security							
Q2: Male (A)	42.86% 66	41.56% 64	6.49% 10	8.44% 13	0.65% 1	52.56% 154	1.82
Q2: Female (B)	39.86% 55	43.48% 60	9.42% 13	6.52% 9	0.72% 1	47.10% 138	1.85
Cost							
Q2: Male (A)	37.42% 58	54.84% 85	1.29% 2	6.45% 10	0.00% 0	52.90% 155	1.77
Q2: Female (B)	39.13% 54	55.80% 77	0.72% 1	3.62% 5	0.72% 1	47.10% 138	1.71
Features							
Q2: Male (A)	63.23% 98 B	34.84% 54 B	0.65% 1	1.29% 2	0.00% 0	52.90% 155	1.40
Q2: Female (B)	36.96% 51 A	54.35% 75 A	2.90% 4	5.07% 7	0.72% 1	47.10% 138	1.78
Brand							
Q2: Male (A)	10.97% 17	39.35% 61 B	5.81% 9 B	36.13% 56	7.74% 12	52.90% 155	2.90
Q2: Female (B)	6.52% 9	28.26% 39 A	13.77% 19 A	38.41% 53	13.04% 18	47.10% 138	3.23

Table 18 Elements Gender

Interestingly contrary to literature respondents from both genders said security was “important” or “very Important” when buying a technological device connectable to the internet. Cost was also considered “important” by both. While the features of the product are “very important” for Men and “important” for Women. Also Interesting is the fact that Women consider Brand to be “less Important” where as a tiny majority of Men say its “very important” or important”.

Q16: I would be willing to give out more personal information in exchange for better value offered:

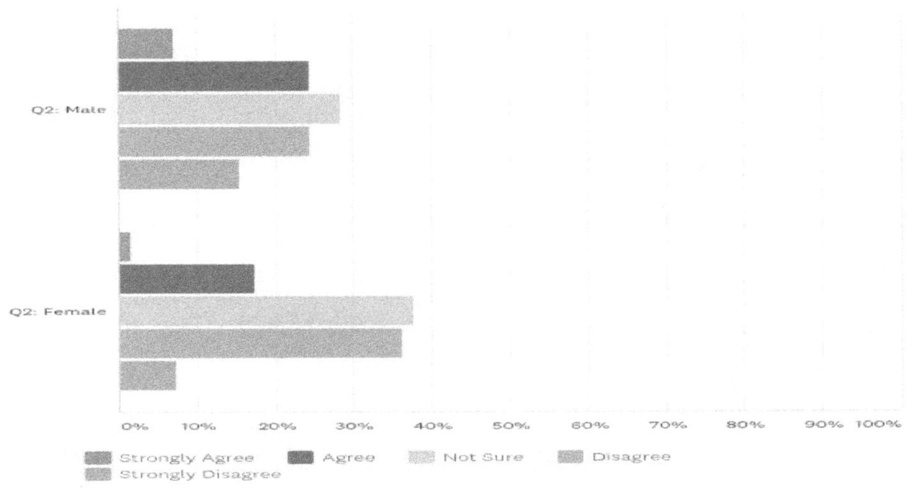

Figure 36 Value Offered Gender

Majority of people from both Genders (men 40 %, women 43%) said (Disagree + Strongly Disagree) they would NOT be willing to give out more information in return for better value offered.

Q17: In terms of buying technological products belonging to the following segments, I would be:

	VERY INTERESTED	INTERESTED	NOT SURE	LESS INTERESTED	NOT INTERESTED	TOTAL	WEIGHTED AVERAGE
Health and Fitness							
Q2: Male (A)	17.42% 27	41.29% 64	10.97% 17	21.29% 33	9.03% 14	52.90% 155	2.63
Q2: Female (B)	18.25% 25	48.91% 67	8.03% 11	18.25% 25	6.57% 9	46.76% 137	2.46
Home Appliances							
Q2: Male (A)	18.71% 29	48.39% 75	11.61% 18	16.13% 25 B	5.16% 8	52.90% 155	2.41
Q2: Female (B)	12.32% 17	40.58% 56	13.77% 19	26.09% 36 A	7.25% 10	47.10% 138	2.75
Home Security							
Q2: Male (A)	25.32% 39	41.56% 64	15.58% 24	11.69% 18	5.84% 9	52.56% 154	2.31
Q2: Female (B)	29.20% 40	34.31% 47	14.60% 20	17.52% 24	4.38% 6	46.76% 137	2.34
Automobiles							
Q2: Male (A)	33.55% 52 B	40.65% 63 B	5.16% 8 B	14.84% 23 B	5.81% 9 B	52.90% 155	2.19
Q2: Female (B)	13.14% 18 A	27.01% 37 A	13.87% 19 A	30.66% 42 A	15.33% 21 A	46.76% 137	3.08

Table 19 Interests Gender

Interestingly, Women are less interested or not interested in the Automotive Segment whereas Men are "Very Interested" or "Interested". Both Share similar interests in other segments. Men show high interests in Home security and Home Appliances. Women show high interests in Home security and health and fitness.

Q18: With regards to technology, I am familiar with products belonging to the following segments:

Health and Fitness	YES	NO	TOTAL	WEIGHTED AVERAGE
Q2: Male (A)	70.97% 110	29.03% 45	52.90% 155	1.29
Q2: Female (B)	78.26% 108	21.74% 30	47.10% 138	1.22
Home Appliances	YES	NO	TOTAL	WEIGHTED AVERAGE
Q2: Male (A)	72.90% 113 B	27.10% 42 B	52.90% 155	1.27
Q2: Female (B)	59.85% 82 A	40.15% 55 A	46.76% 137	1.40
Home Security	YES	NO	TOTAL	WEIGHTED AVERAGE
Q2: Male (A)	65.58% 101 B	34.42% 53 B	52.56% 154	1.34
Q2: Female (B)	50.00% 68 A	50.00% 68 A	46.42% 136	1.50
Automobiles	YES	NO	TOTAL	WEIGHTED AVERAGE
Q2: Male (A)	77.42% 120 B	22.58% 35 B	52.90% 155	1.23
Q2: Female (B)	58.52% 79 A	41.48% 56 A	46.08% 135	1.41

Table 20 Familiarity - Gender

Mostly, both Genders are familiar with all the listed segments of IoT, however, Health and Fitness is the most familiar for the Women whereas the Automotive section is most familiar with the Men.

6) Discussion

Overall results of the study came out somewhat surprising, in this chapter the important findings will be highlighted and compared with the literature.

Consumer Awareness

- The consumer awareness has increased overtime. Also, today people (63 %) are more familiar with the term Internet of Things as compared to previous studies. It is entirely possible that the events of the past two years, and the news surrounding hacking scandals has led to this increased awareness.
- Gender has an influence on consumer awareness of IoT Vulnerabilities, men are more aware than women. Work must be done to bridge this gap.
- (92%) of respondents said more work should be done by the industry and the government to increase the understanding and education of consumers.
- While most men believe all their devices connectable to the internet are secure, most of the women said they were "Not Sure" about it.
- For the consumers of Austria and India at least, Nationality has no influence on their awareness rather the awareness of IoT is on a similar level.

Overall it can be said that there has been a shift in the consumer awareness on cyber security towards a positive side as it has increased. The increased awareness suggests that with the changing face of technology, and now with the increased media scrutiny, consumers are also evolving and becoming more aware. Which is why the previous research we read in the literature had different outcomes towards awareness.

Perception of Privacy

- Overall there is a "Negative" perception of privacy, with most respondents (53%) saying that trust in technology has decreased.

- Majority (86%) said that they are careful about giving out confidential information when using technological products which suggest people try to do everything in their power (that they know of) to remain secure.
- Complacency persists on the part of the consumers, when talking about taking protective measures around connectable devices and application, most (53%) said they do so only “sometimes”. Perhaps they are not familiar with the protective measures they could take. Again, a lack of education about IoT and Cyber Security points out here.
- Despite the growing distrust and privacy concerns, most people (44%) will still not be discouraged from buying technological products, highlighting the dependence on technology of the society.
- Most people (43%) feel there is enough media coverage surrounding hacking and security breaches. Even though media coverage for such events is a new phenomenon, probably, people are still adjusting to it.

Like the literature suggest, Trust will be an issue going forward with technology however it will still not stop people from buying technological products.

Value Perception

- Gender has an Influence on value perception, which is understandable as most men and women have differing levels and types of interests when it comes to technology. IoT associated products remain popular and most people expect to make purchases in the coming years.
- Security is valued! Most people (69%) said they will agree to pay extra for a more secure product. Companies can profit by prioritizing security in their product development.
- Nationality also has an influence on value perception, for Indian and Austrian. Indians are more eager to pay extra for security than Austrian. Indians also consider Security, Features and Brand as far more essential elements to consider when buying a technological product. For Austrian,

Security and Feature are important but not as much as Indian, while they are less interested in the Brand of the products. Cost has a similar importance level for both.

- Most Indians (39%) will be willing to give out additional information in exchange for better value offered, whereas most Austrian will not be.
- As described in the literature, Health and Fitness remains the most popular segment, especially with women. Men show high interests in Home security and Home Appliances. Additionally, men would be interested in the Automotive sector, whereas women are not too keen.
- Home Appliances is a popular segment with Indians. While Austrian are less interested in Automobiles. Both are interested in Health and Fitness and Home Security.
- If the consumers are familiar with a segment, that does not guarantee that they would be interested in it as well.

6.1) Conclusion

The difference seen in the results of the study compared to the findings from the literature show that IoT is a continuously evolving field, however, the consumers are also evolving and becoming more aware of technology. Which means the dynamics of the consumer and IoT relationship are different now as compared to what they were 2-3 years ago.

In just the past year alone, with the US elections and other major hacking scandals, it appears the people are starting to become more informed about the issue which explains why the outcome especially regarding awareness is different to the similar studies of the past or maybe Austria and India are different than US and UK, with people being more informed about these issues in the former two. The age of the respondents is also important to take under consideration, as most of the respondents belong to a younger generation (less than 35 years). Which explains of the sudden interest and alertness to cyber security vulnerabilities. It is entirely possible, that if the same study were to be conducted with an older population group, the results be vastly different. Despite the security concerns of the consumers and the increased awareness to those threats, the products/services associated with Internet of things are expected to prosper in the coming years. With the leading segments to be Health and Fitness, Home Appliance, Home Security and Automobiles which coincides with the findings form the literature as well. People also value security and are willing to pay extra for it.

While in the literature, the security vulnerabilities are not just down to the technical flaws, it has a lot to do with the complacency of the end users. People seem to be aware of the connectable devices around them, when it comes to knowing about how many devices they own. After the results of this study, it appears that most people have finally woken up to the threats and are in a more secure position (at least from their viewpoint) as compared to a few years ago. But this could be the perfect time for the industry to win back the trust of the consumers by reaching out to them and talking about security and protective measure. While it is also the responsibility of the government to run campaigns or education programs to bridge the gap between consumer and industry in understanding Internet of Things and cyber security. It will serve the society well in the coming years, as Internet of Things reaches its true potential.

7) Limitations and Implication for Future Research

This chapter talks about the limitations of the study and the implications for the future research.

7.1) Limitations

The big limitation of the study concerns with time and resource. Due to which the length of the survey and number of respondents becomes restricted. Due to the vastness of the topic, it would have been better to go deeper into in and ask more question of the consumers to have an in-depth understanding. There was a lack of literature available based on the selected countries of Indian and Austria. Which is why most of this research has been based on a much broader spectrum of previous researched conducted. Lastly, although it is entirely possible to get a better understating by increasing the scope of the study, the author is not certain if that would change the outcome or the results drastically.

7.2) Implication for Future Research

Some of the important question and topic were left out of the research due to a restriction of resources. These include the legislative aspect surrounding Internet of Things. Are there enough laws in place to safeguard the consumers? It should be made sure that there no longer exist any "grey areas" when it comes to the legislative cover for cyber-crime. Moreover, it would be interesting to learn about the economic impacts of IoT on the economies of Indian and Austria, considering jobs and businesses will be greatly affected by it. After understanding the specific needs of the consumer base in terms of Gender, it would make sense to do research on how best to market those products to the people. IoT services will change along with the advent of innovative vulnerabilities and threats. Further research and development is required to fight the threats and vulnerabilities. Expect IoT and cyber security to remain as an active area of research for the foreseeable future.

Bibliography

(NCSA) National Cyber Security Alliance, & ESET . (2016). *OUR INCREASINGLY CONNECTED LIVES.* ESET.

Accenture. (2014). *The Internet of Things : The Future of Consumer Adoption.* The Acquity Group .

BBC. (2017). *Russia hacking claims: Trump says no effect on election.* BBC.

BERTINO, E., CHOO, K.-K. R., GEORGAKOPOLOUS, D., & NEPAL, S. (2016). Internet of Things (IoT): Smart and Secure Service Delivery. *ACM Transactions on Internet Technology.*

Bhattacharya, A. (2017). *The Internet of Things could be the light at the end of the tunnel for Indian IT.* Quartz India.

Biggs, P., Garrity, J., LaSalle, C., & Polomska, A. (2016). *Harnessing IoT Global Development.* Geneva: ITU.

Boulton, C. (2016, August 5). *IoT security suffers from a lack of awareness.* Retrieved from http://www.cio.com: http://www.cio.com/article/3104116/internet-of-things/iot-security-suffers-from-a-lack-of-awareness.html

BullGuard. (2017, January 4). *http://www.thewindowsclub.com/secure-internet-things-iot-devices-pdf-guide.* Retrieved from http://www.thewindowsclub.com: http://www.thewindowsclub.com/secure-internet-things-iot-devices-pdf-guide

Canonical. (2017, January 30). *https://insights.ubuntu.com.* Retrieved from https://insights.ubuntu.com: https://insights.ubuntu.com/2017/01/30/48-of-people-unaware-their-iot-devices-pose-a-security-threat/

Clerck, J.-P. D. (n.d.). *IoT security and the consumer: the challenges and education question.* i-SCOOP.

Internet of Things Research Study. Hewlett-Packard Development Company Company, H.-P. D. (2014).

India ahead of several markets in iot adoption to improve customer experience (2017, March 14). *Genesys.* Retrieved from http://computer.expressbpd.com: http://computer.expressbpd.com/news/india-ahead-of-several-markets-in-iot-adoption-to-improve-customer-experience-genesys/20831/

Davies, R. (2015). *The Internet of Things Opportunities and challenges.* European Parliamentary Research Service.

Frick, S. (2016). *Internet of Things: For Business Compulsory.* SAP News Center.

Groopman, J. (2015). *Consumer Perceptions Privacy IoT .* Altimeter Group.

hindustantimes. (2017). *From Britain to India, massive ransomware attack creates havoc.* New Delhi: hindustantimes.

ISACA. (2015). *ISACA Survey.* Rolling Meadows, IL: ISACA.

ISACA. (2015). *ISACA Survey.* Rolling Meadows, IL, USA: ISACA.

James Manyika, M. C. (2015). *Unlocking the potential of the Internet of Things.* McKinsey Global Institute.

LLP, E. &. (2011). *The Digitization of Everything.* U.K: Ernst and Young LLP.

Lueth, K. L. (2014). *IoT market segments – Biggest opportunities in industrial manufacturing.* IoT-analytics.

Lueth, K. L. (2014). *IoT market segments 'Biggest opportunities in industrial manufacturing'.* IoT ANALYTICS.

Manyika, J., Chui, M., Bisson, P., Woetze, J., Dobbs, R., Bughin, J., & Aharon , D. (2015). *Unlocking the potential of the Internet of Things.* McKinsey Global Institute.

Meola, A. (2016). How the Internet of Things will affect security & privacy. *TECH INSIDER.*

Morris, D. Z. (2017). *Hackers Hijack Hotel's Smart Locks, Demand Ransom.* fortune.

MSV, J. (2016). Security Is Fast Becoming The Achilles Heel of Consumer Internet of Things. *forbes.*

Newman, P. (2017). *The Internet of Things Report.* Business Insider.

PRNewswire. (2017, April 2017). *India Internet of Things Market By Component, By Communication Technology, Competition Forecast and Opportunities, 2012-2022.* Retrieved from http://www.prnewswire.com/: http://www.prnewswire.com/news-releases/india-internet-of-things-market-by-component-by-communication-technology-competition-forecast-and-opportunities-2012-2022-300439121.html

Roman, R., Zhou, J., & Lopez, J. (2013). *On the features and challenges of security and privacy in distributed internet of things.* Computer Networks.

SACMAT. (2016). Security and Privacy in the Age of Internet of Things: Opportunities and Challenges. *SACMAT'16.* Shanghai: ACM ISBN 978-1-4503-3802-8/16/06.

Saunders, M., Lewis, P., & Thornhill, A. (2009). *Research methods for Business Students 5th edition.* Harlow, Essex: Pearson Education.

Schneider, R. (2016). *Enhance IoT Security & Optimize Data with a VPN.* EMnify.

Security, I. (2016). *McAfee Most Hackable Holiday Gifts.* Intel.

Sicari, S., Rizzardi, A., Grieco, L., & Coen-Porisini, A. (2014). *Security, privacy and trust in Internet of Things: The road ahead.* Italy: Elsevier.

Sniderman, B., & Raynor, M. (2015). *How to build value for customers with the Internet of Things.* Deloitte. Digital.

Solon , O., & Hern, A. (2017). *'Petya' ransomware attack: what is it and how can it be stopped?* London: The Guardian.

Weber, R. H. (2010). *Internet of Things – New security and privacy challenges.* ScienceDirect .

Weissman, C. G. (2015). *BI Intelligence survey of technology executives.* Business Insider.

Wheelwright, G. (2016). How 2016 became the year of the hack – and what it means for the future. *The Guardian*.

Wilson, H. J., Shah, B., & Whipple, B. (2015). *How People Are Actually Using the Internet of Things.* HBR.

Ziegeldorf, J. H., Morchon, O. G., & Wehrle, K. (2013). *Privacy in the Internet of Things: threats.* Wiley Online Library.

Ziegeldorf, J. H., Morchon, O. G., & Wehrle, K. (2013). *Privacy in the Internet of Things: Threats and Challenges.* Aachen: SECURITY AND COMMUNICATION NETWORKS.

Appendix

Transcript from the Interviews

The Following is a Transcript of the Interview done with Professor Michael Brickmann

Brief Introduction

DI (FH) Michael Brickmann MA is a Full Professor at the FH Joanneum in Graz, Austria. He is on the academic staff for Internet Technology (Bachelor), Software Design (Bachelor) and IT Law and Management (Master).

Contact Info

Interview

1. **What is your general idea of IoT technology? What is your perception of IoT progression?**

   "It has been quite fast, and it is not so surprising."

2. **Do you feel there are security risks that come with the adaptation of IoT technology and which area or devices do you feel are more vulnerable? (transfer between devices, stored data, what are the problems exactly what are the fault lines in a technological sense)**

   "Yes, security is a concern, and nothing can be complete secure. Getting data into the internet, because all data is variable, and it can be stolen and sold easily so that is quite a security concern. Also, this can be down to the fact that there is poor coding/encryption of the software making it an easy target. "

3. **Gap between understanding technology and common man is increasing? Even though there is an increased involvement of technology in our everyday life?**

   "Yes, I feel it is, people are more consumption oriented and are more focused on acquiring a certain product rather understanding how it works. People should be clever and ask questions, the developers also have the responsibility to make the product/service as secure as possible and I would say it is more of a shared responsibility."

4. **What are the best ways to secure a device from a technological perspective? Is inscription sufficient and is the cost of the inscription a hindrance for companies?**

   "Technology is not ready for state of the art tools like a retina scan to be implemented on a broader level as that can be too expensive. But even if it was done it does not mean it is completely secure like a said before that can be hacked as well. Maybe down the line we see technology like a heartbeat sensor but that is not ready yet for a broader level."

5. **Would we come to a situation like this where all the devices connected to the internet would need to be secured separately? If yes, is that not difficult and quite confusing for a common man? (Some Experts suggest different passwords for different devices.)**

   "Yes, that would be very confusing and highly inconvenient. But yes, that is one way of securing devices for now."

6. **As we move quickly into the age of IoT, do feel we are very under prepared? In general, technological processes does security enters the product development simultaneously or is it somewhere down the line?**

   "No, security techniques are evolving as well but not fully implementable, providing security can be expensive as well. Regarding product development, security concerns are considered hand in hand and it is not an afterthought.

I would say speaking of Austria and other developed nation on a Global scale the state is the same, the people are not prepared but the countries are. For Austria, I can say we have security forum of Austria where these things are discussed and other E-business and IT related topic as well and I believe we are going down the right path".

7. **Do you feel the target audience is aware of the security risks that come with IoT? If yes, what can be done to re-assure them.**

   "Talking about Austrian people I would say in my opinion Austrian people are not aware about cyber security concerns. It should be taken more seriously, but right now the older people are not sure whether are going to use technology and gadgets, the younger ones are trying it out thinking they are untouchable."

8. **Do you feel there is a GAP between the general population and the industry when it comes to knowing the security aspects of IoT? Why do feel that GAP exists.**

   "Yes, there is definitely a GAP that exists between the population and the industry. Not just concerning the IoT but I think cyber security. And I think this down to a lack of effort on both ends. The industry should do more to make the people more aware, whereas the people should also put in more effort."

9. **Do you feel security is an afterthought in the field of IOT or has it been well thought off and pre-planned?**

   "No, it comes in the discussion quite early in the development process. Not an afterthought for sure!"

10. **What would you say are the most important-issues that need to be addressed within the realm of IoT?**

    "I think security is important and, I to make people more aware about the risks associated with this type of technology."

11. **What impact can we expect from IoT technology in the next 5 years?**

"I see a lot on IoT devises coming to the market, there is a time of IOT boom. Down the line there is a possibility of even more security problems has there will be a lot more variables to deal with. A lot more data for serves to handle."

12. **Considering the impact IoT will have in the future, do you feel people are aware of what is about to hit them?**

    "I do think people are starting to gain more knowledge about these type of things as the hear more and more about hacking scandals and security breaches, but yes still overall, I would say the majority is not very aware."

13. **Do you feel consumer awareness is on par with the impact the IoT is expected to have?**

    "I am not sure, but I am guessing it is not."

14. **Do you feel the benefits of our interconnectivity, go hand in hand with the risks of being compromised/hacked? If their risks and benefits which one prevails?**

    "Depends on the devise and the person using it. Risks are higher for most devise, but it is also because of the over consuming attitude of the people who are not clever enough to know about the risks."

15. **What are the solution that you feel could be implemented to cater to these risks?**

    "Maybe more laws should be introduced to have a more generalž7basic standard to be followed by the developers. That could maybe also prove to be a hindrance to technological innovation especially for smaller independent developers."

16. **Should there be more work done by the Government? How do you see its role in all of this?**

    "Yes, Governments should be more involved, there should be and active approach rather than a reactive one. There can be an industry standard to be followed to stay up to date and state of the art, this could be expensive but more secure. But in Austria the government is doing a lot and making sure to be as safe as possible when it comes to cyber security. Government itself is very secure for these threats, it has layers of security in its network, but it is also important to make the internet and IOT safe for the public."

<u>The Following is a Transcript of the Interview done with Professor Marko Bajec</u>

Brief Introduction

Marko Bajec is a Full Professor at the Faculty of Computer & Information Science, University of Ljubljana. He is Head of the Laboratory for Data Technologies and head of IoT Demo Centre. His research interests focus on IT and data Governance including information retrieval, web search and extraction, data integration, data management, data analysis, software development methods, IT/IS strategy planning. In his career, he has led or coordinated over 30 applied and research projects. For his contribution in transferring knowledge to industry he received several awards and recognitions.

Contact Info

Interview

1. **What is your general idea of IoT technology? What is your perception of IOT progression?**

   "I am very Impressed by the progression of the IOT. It is very promising and has seen a lot of investments in recent years, so the expectations are high. We hear nowadays these terms like "smart cities", "smart health" etc which means that IOT is becoming more popular. However, the one thing that is a bit concerning is that the fact that the progression has been fast perhaps TOO fast."

2. **Do you feel there are security risks that come with the adaptation of IOT technology and which area or devices do you feel are more vulnerable? (transfer between devices, stored data, what are the problems exactly what are the fault lines in a technological sense)**

   "Security is the biggest concern of the IOT. Most devices are small and the thing with making a device secure is the fact that they require large energy so a powerful processor. But the problem with IOT is the fact that most devices used are "smart devices" which means low power low energy but inexpensive products which makes them attractive to the consumer at the same time but yeah, they are no secure at all but affordable. Data sharing is the most venerable thing right now and the way it is been done is also a problem. There needs to be more security added to that."

3. **Gap between understanding technology and common man is increasing? Even though there is an increased involvement of technology in our everyday life?**

   "The Gap is the same for me if not lessened, because we are in a situation now when these things specially the IOT is effecting our lives more, so we are talking about it more, so I would say we are more aware."

4. **What are the best ways to secure a device from a technological perspective? Is inscription sufficient and is the cost of the inscription a hindrance for companies?**

   "I would say that security standards first lie with the company, that they try to make as much of a secure product as possible. However, they also need to keep in mind the user friendliness. But the thing is, we have technology to make it more secure, but it's are more expensive so are harder to integrate with products, especially for independent companies who do not have a lot of capital. Also, most companies who are selling products make them wireless but then again wireless products are low energy and low power which also makes them less secure."

5. **Would we come to a situation like this where all the devices connected to the internet would need to be secured separately? If yes, is that not difficult and quite confusing for a common man? (Some Experts suggest different passwords for different devices.)**

   "I think we have that situation today to some extent, but it is not down to the fact that we do not have enough security tools to make it different rather it is because of the cost of providing security to different devices especially which are cheap to buy."

6. **As we move quickly into the age of IOT, do feel we are very under prepared? In general, technological processes does security enters the product development simultaneously or is it somewhere down the line?**

   "Security is developed parallel to the products and that's how it usually goes. But yes, for IOT specifically there still seem to be a lot of concerns regarding security but that should be addressed soon with more innovations."

7. **Do you feel security is an afterthought in the field of IoT or has it been well thought off and pre-planned?**

   "I certainly feel that the progression has been quite rapid, but the security is always planned parallel to technological innovations, so I do not think it is an afterthought, but it is proving to be harder to implement on a broader/societal level".

8. **What would you say are the most important-issues that need to be addressed within the realm of IoT?**

   "I would say security is the major concern at this moment and how to provide it in a way which keeps the devices affordable and the industry profitable."

9. **What impact can we expect from IoT technology in the next 5 years?**

   "I feel like right now it is a boom, it is expected to keep on growing for the next 5 years and then we might see some stability and maturity. "

10. **Considering the impact IoT will have in the future, do you feel people are aware of what is about to hit them?**

    "I can't say for sure, we are living in the time of a change and more technologically aware generation. "

11. **Do you feel consumer awareness is on par with the impact the IoT is expected to have?**

    "I feel we need consumer associations to make more awareness, like we did with GMO (Genetically Modified Organisms). It should be a step by step process to bring people closer to the understanding of the products."

12. **Do you feel the benefits of our interconnectivity, go hand in hand with the risks of being compromised/hacked? If their risks and benefits which one prevails?**

    "Look nothing is ever completely secure so we will always have to worry about being hacked but we cannot stop with innovation and should rather takes both things (technological advancement and security) hand in hand. "

13. **What are the solution that you feel could be implemented to cater to these risks?**

    "Well it depends on devise to devise but yeah maybe there could be better data encryption, so it is harder to crack and better security protocol. There are a lot on things that can be done and even are possible today but again it's the problem of implementing it on a broader level keeping the cost in check."

14. **Should Governments play a more significant role in providing cybersecurity?**

    "Yes! Governments should play a more key role, but the problem is we are yet to define some sort of industry standards that can then be enforced on a national level. And it is not so easy to set standards."

Complete Hypothesis

Awareness

RQ A: How does Gender influence the consumer awareness of the internet of things?

6. I am Familiar with the term Internet of Things.

   H0: Gender does not influence the familiarity with the term Internet of Things.

   H1: Gender does influence the familiarity with the term Internet of Things.

7. How many devices connectable to the internet do I own?

   H0: Gender does not influence the number of connectable devices owned by people.

   H1: Gender does influence the number of connectable devices owned by people.

8. All my devices connectable to the internet are secure.

   H0: Gender does not influence the perceived security of devices connectable to the internet.

   H1: Gender does influence the perceived security of devices connectable to the internet.

9. I regularly update all my devices connectable to the internet.

   H0: Gender does not influence the likely hood of updating devices connectable to the internet.

   H1: Gender does influence the likely hood of updating devices connectable to the internet.

10. More work should be done by the IT industry and the government to educate consumers about internet security.

H0: Gender does not influence the perception of consumer education with regards to internet security.

H1: Gender does influence the perception of consumer education with regards to internet security.

RQ B: How does Nationality influence the consumer awareness of the internet of things?

1. I am Familiar with the term Internet of Things.

   H0: Nationality does not influence the familiarity with the term Internet of Things.

   H1: Nationality does influence the familiarity with the term Internet of Things.

2. How many devices connectable to the internet do I own?

   H0: Nationality does not influence the number of connectable devices owned by people

   H1: Gender does influence the number of connectable devices owned by people

3. All my devices connectable to the internet are secure.

   H0: Nationality does not influence the perceived security of devices connectable to the internet.

   H1: Nationality does influence the perceived security of devices connectable to the internet.

4. I regularly update all my devices connectable to the internet.

   H0: Nationality does not influence the likely hood of updating devices connectable to the internet.

   H1: Nationality does influence the likely hood of updating devices connectable to the internet.

5. More work should be done by the IT industry and the government to educate consumers about internet security.

H0: Nationality does not influence the perception of consumer education with regards to internet security.

H1: Nationality does influence the perception of consumer education with regards to internet security.

Privacy

RQ A: How does Gender influence the perception of privacy towards the internet of things?

1. I take protective measures around technological products (For example covering the camera on my laptop)

   H0: Gender does not influence protective behaviour around technological products.

   H1: Gender does influence protective behaviour around technological products.

2. I am discouraged from buying connectable devices due to security and privacy concerns

   H0: Gender does not influence the tendency to buy connectable devices due to security and privacy concerns.

   H1: Gender does influence the tendency to buy connectable devices due to security and privacy concerns.

3. When using applications or devices connectable to the internet I am careful about giving out personal information.

   H0: Gender does not influence the tendency to givie out personal information on connectable devices.

   H1: Gender does influence the tendency to givie out personal information on connectable devices.

4. I think there is enough media coverage of attacks involving hacking and security breaches with regards to the Internet.

H0: Gender does not influence perception about media coverage of attacks involving hacking and security breaches with regards to the Internet.

H1: Gender does influence perception about media coverage of attacks involving hacking and security breaches with regards to the Internet.

5. I think trust in technology by the consumers has decreased over time.
   H0: Gender does not influence the level of trust in technology by the consumers had over time.

   H1: Gender does influence the level of trust in technology by the consumers had over time.

RQ B: How does Nationality influence the perception of privacy towards the internet of things?

1. I take protective measures around technological products (For example covering the camera on my laptop).
   H0: Nationality does not influence protective behaviour around technological products.

   H1: Nationality does influence protective behaviour around technological products.

2. I am discouraged from buying connectable devices due to security and privacy concerns.
   H0: Nationality does not influence the tendency to buy connectable devices due to security and privacy concerns

   H1: Nationality does influence the tendency to buy connectable devices due to security and privacy concerns

3. When using applications or devices connectable to the internet I am careful about giving out personal information.

H0: Nationality does not influence the tendency to give out personal information on connectable devices.

H1: Nationality does influence the tendency to give out personal information on connectable devices.

4. I think there is enough media coverage of attacks involving hacking and security breaches with regards to the Internet.

   H0: Nationality does not influence perception about media coverage of attacks involving hacking and security breaches with regards to the Internet.

   H1: Nationality does influence perception about media coverage of attacks involving hacking and security breaches with regards to the Internet.

5. I think trust in technology by the consumers has decreased over time.

   H0: Nationality does not influence the level of trust in technology by the consumers over time.

   H1: Nationality does influence the level of trust in technology by the consumers over time.

Value

RQA: Does being the national of a different country cause a difference in the respondents' value perception with regards to Internet of Things technology?

H0: There is no difference in terms of perceived value with regards to Internet of Things technology between respondents of Austria and India.

H1: There is a difference in terms of perceived value with regards to Internet of Things technology between respondents of Austria and India.

RQB: Does the demographic variable gender cause a difference in respondents' value perception with regards to Internet of Things technology?

H0: There is no difference in terms of perceived value with regards to Internet of Things technology between men and women respondents.

H1: There is a difference in terms of perceived value with regards to Internet of Things technology between men and women respondents.

Survey

Consumers and the Internet of Things

Survey about consumer awareness and perception of Internet of Things (IoT)

Introduction

Dear Participant!

Thank you for taking part in the following survey, which will take about 8-10 minutes of your time.

My name is Mashood Hassan Qureshi and I am conducting a research project within the scope of my master thesis with the title Security and Internet of Things (IoT): Analysing the difference between Austria and India in consumer awareness of IoT Vulnerabilities, Perception towards IoT Privacy and Value. The aim of this online questionnaire is to get a profound understanding consumers' knowledge of Internet of Things and their position on certain aspects relating to security, privacy and value. Internet of Things IoT is a term used to describe 'A worldwide network of interconnected entities', a large number of smart devices, that interact with each other to collaborate in achieving a common goal.

Confidentially Agreement

The author hereby confirms, the data collected through this survey will be kept confidential and stored in an electronic format.

The results of this will form the basis of the section on empirical research of my work. Please feel free to contact me (mashood.hassan@edu.fh-joanneum.at) if you want to be informed about the results.

Yours sincerely,

Mashood Hassan Qureshi
FH-Joanneum
Graz, Austria

Consumers and the Internet of Things

Please provide the following personal details:

* 1. Indicate your nationality.

- ◯ Austrian
- ◯ Indian
- ◯ Other (please specify)

* 2. Indicate your gender.

- ◯ Male
- ◯ Female

* 3. Indicate your age.

Consumers and the Internet of Things

Awareness

Please answer the following questions :

* 1. I am familiar with the term Internet of things (IoT)

- ◯ Yes
- ◯ No
- ◯ Not Sure

* 2. How many devices connectable to the internet do I own?

- ◯ 1-3
- ◯ 3-5
- ◯ 5 or more
- ◯ Not Sure

* 3. All my devices connectable to the internet are secure.

◯ Strongly Agree ◯ Agree ◯ Not Sure ◯ Disagree ◯ Strongly Disagree

4. I regularly update all my devices connectable to the internet.

◯ Strongly Agree ◯ Agree ◯ Not Sure ◯ Disagree ◯ Strongly Disagree

5. More work should be done by the IT industry and the government to educate consumers about internet security.

◯ Strongly Agree ◯ Agree ◯ Not Sure ◯ Disagree ◯ Strongly Disagree

Consumers and the Internet of Things

Perception towards Privacy

Please answer the following questions :

* 1. I take protective measures around technological products (For example covering the camera on my laptop)

Always Sometimes Never

2. I am discouraged from buying connectable devices due to security and privacy concerns

Strongly Agree Agree Not Sure Disagree Strongly Disagree

* 3. When using applications or devices connectable to the internet I am careful about giving out personal information.

Strongly Agree Agree Not Sure Disagree Strongly Disagree

* 4. I think there is enough media coverage of attacks involving hacking and security breaches with regards to the Internet.

Strongly Agree Agree Not Sure Disagree Strongly Disagree

5. I think trust in technology by the consumers has decreased over time.

Strongly Agree Agree Not Sure Disagree Strongly Disagree

Consumers and the Internet of Things

Value Perception

Please answer the following questions :

* 1. I would be willing to pay extra for a technological product that has better security

○ Strongly Agree ○ Agree ○ Not Sure ○ Disagree ○ Strongly Disagree

2. When buying technological product, I consider the following elements to be :

	Very Important	Important	Not Sure	less Important	Not Important
Security	○	○	○	○	○
Cost	○	○	○	○	○
Features	○	○	○	○	○
Brand	○	○	○	○	○

* 3. I would be willing to give out more personal information in exchange for better value offered :

○ Strongly Agree ○ Agree ○ Not Sure ○ Disagree ○ Strongly Disagree

* 4. In terms of buying technological products belonging to the following segments, I would be :

	Very Interested	Interested	Not Sure	Less Interested	Not Interested
Health and Fitness	○	○	○	○	○
Home Appliances	○	○	○	○	○
Home Security	○	○	○	○	○
Automobiles	○	○	○	○	○

5. With regards to technology, I am familiar with products belonging to the following segments :

	Yes	No
Health and Fitness	○	○
Home Appliances	○	○
Home Security	○	○
Automobiles	○	○

SPSS

Frequencies

Indicate your nationality.

		Frequency	Percent	Valid Percent	Cumulative Percent
Valid	Other (please specify)	42	14.0	14.0	14.0
	Austrian	157	52.3	52.3	66.3
	Indian	101	33.7	33.7	100.0
	Total	300	100.0	100.0	

Indicate your gender.

		Frequency	Percent	Valid Percent	Cumulative Percent
Valid	Male	160	53.3	53.3	53.3
	Female	140	46.7	46.7	100.0
	Total	300	100.0	100.0	

I am familiar with the term Internet of things (IoT)

		Frequency	Percent	Valid Percent	Cumulative Percent
Valid	Yes	183	61.0	63.1	63.1
	No	65	21.7	22.4	85.5
	Not Sure	42	14.0	14.5	100.0
	Total	290	96.7	100.0	

How many devices connectable to the internet do I own?

		Frequency	Percent	Valid Percent	Cumulative Percent
Valid	1-3	146	48.7	50.3	50.3
	3-5	85	28.3	29.3	79.7
	5 or more	55	18.3	19.0	98.6
	Not Sure	4	1.3	1.4	100.0
	Total	290	96.7	100.0	

All my devices connectable to the internet are secure.

		Frequency	Percent	Valid Percent	Cumulative Percent
Valid	Strongly Agree	14	4.7	4.8	4.8
	Agree	111	37.0	38.3	43.1
	Not Sure	121	40.3	41.7	84.8
	Disagree	41	13.7	14.1	99.0
	Strongly Disagree	3	1.0	1.0	100.0
	Total	290	96.7	100.0	

I regularly update all my devices connectable to the internet.

		Frequency	Percent	Valid Percent	Cumulative Percent
Valid	Strongly Agree	70	23.3	24.2	24.2
	Agree	152	50.7	52.6	76.8
	Not Sure	24	8.0	8.3	85.1
	Disagree	42	14.0	14.5	99.7
	Strongly Disagree	1	.3	.3	100.0
	Total	289	96.3	100.0	

More work should be done by the IT industry and the government to educate consumers about internet security.

		Frequency	Percent	Valid Percent	Cumulative Percent
Valid	Strongly Agree	167	55.7	57.8	57.8
	Agree	101	33.7	34.9	92.7
	Not Sure	12	4.0	4.2	96.9
	Disagree	6	2.0	2.1	99.0
	Strongly Disagree	3	1.0	1.0	100.0
	Total	289	96.3	100.0	

I take protective measures around technological products (For example covering the camera on my laptop)

		Frequency	Percent	Valid Percent	Cumulative Percent
Valid	Always	67	22.3	23.4	23.4
	Sometimes	151	50.3	52.8	76.2
	Never	68	22.7	23.8	100.0
	Total	286	95.3	100.0	

I am discouraged from buying connectable devices due to security and privacy concerns

		Frequency	Percent	Valid Percent	Cumulative Percent
Valid	Strongly Agree	18	6.0	6.3	6.3
	Agree	70	23.3	24.5	30.8
	Not Sure	70	23.3	24.5	55.2
	Disagree	109	36.3	38.1	93.4
	Strongly Disagree	19	6.3	6.6	100.0
	Total	286	95.3	100.0	

When using applications or devices connectable to the internet I am careful about giving out personal information.

		Frequency	Percent	Valid Percent	Cumulative Percent
Valid	Strongly Agree	111	37.0	38.8	38.8
	Agree	136	45.3	47.6	86.4
	Not Sure	16	5.3	5.6	92.0
	Disagree	21	7.0	7.3	99.3
	Strongly Disagree	2	.7	.7	100.0
	Total	286	95.3	100.0	

I think there is enough media coverage of attacks involving hacking and security breaches with regards to the Internet.

		Frequency	Percent	Valid Percent	Cumulative Percent
Valid	Strongly Agree	30	10.0	10.5	10.5
	Agree	94	31.3	32.9	43.4
	Not Sure	82	27.3	28.7	72.0
	Disagree	68	22.7	23.8	95.8
	Strongly Disagree	12	4.0	4.2	100.0
	Total	286	95.3	100.0	

I think trust in technology by the consumers has decreased over time.

		Frequency	Percent	Valid Percent	Cumulative Percent
Valid	Strongly Agree	29	9.7	10.1	10.1
	Agree	122	40.7	42.7	52.8
	Not Sure	67	22.3	23.4	76.2
	Disagree	52	17.3	18.2	94.4
	Strongly Disagree	16	5.3	5.6	100.0
Total		300	100.0		

I would be willing to pay extra for a technological product that has better security

		Frequency	Percent	Valid Percent	Cumulative Percent
Valid	Strongly Agree	54	18.0	18.9	18.9
	Agree	145	48.3	50.9	69.8
	Not Sure	47	15.7	16.5	86.3
	Disagree	31	10.3	10.9	97.2
	Strongly Disagree	8	2.7	2.8	100.0
Total		300	100.0		

Security

		Frequency	Percent	Valid Percent	Cumulative Percent
Valid	Very Important	117	39.0	41.2	41.2
	Important	121	40.3	42.6	83.8
	Not Sure	23	7.7	8.1	91.9
	less Important	21	7.0	7.4	99.3
	Not Important	2	.7	.7	100.0
Total		300	100.0		

Cost

		Frequency	Percent	Valid Percent	Cumulative Percent
Valid	Very Important	109	36.3	38.2	38.2
	Important	157	52.3	55.1	93.3
	Not Sure	3	1.0	1.1	94.4
	less Important	15	5.0	5.3	99.6
	Not Important	1	.3	.4	100.0
Total		300	100.0		

Features

		Frequency	Percent	Valid Percent	Cumulative Percent
Valid	Very Important	145	48.3	50.9	50.9
	Important	125	41.7	43.9	94.7
	Not Sure	5	1.7	1.8	96.5
	less Important	9	3.0	3.2	99.6
	Not Important	1	.3	.4	100.0
Total		300	100.0		

Brand

		Frequency	Percent	Valid Percent	Cumulative Percent
Valid	Very Important	25	8.3	8.8	8.8
	Important	98	32.7	34.4	43.2
	Not Sure	28	9.3	9.8	53.0
	less Important	105	35.0	36.8	89.8
	Not Important	29	9.7	10.2	100.0
Total		300	100.0		

I would be willing to give out more personal information in exchange for better value offered:

		Frequency	Percent	Valid Percent	Cumulative Percent
Valid	Strongly Agree	12	4.0	4.2	4.2
	Agree	61	20.3	21.4	25.6
	Not Sure	92	30.7	32.3	57.9
	Disagree	87	29.0	30.5	88.4
	Strongly Disagree	33	11.0	11.6	100.0
Total		300	100.0		

Health and Fitness

		Frequency	Percent	Valid Percent	Cumulative Percent
Valid	Very Interested	50	16.7	17.5	17.5
	Interested	129	43.0	45.3	62.8
	Not Sure	27	9.0	9.5	72.3
	Less Interested	56	18.7	19.6	91.9
	Not Interested	23	7.7	8.1	100.0
Total		300	100.0		

Home Appliances

		Frequency	Percent	Valid Percent	Cumulative Percent
Valid	Very Interested	45	15.0	15.8	15.8
	Interested	128	42.7	44.9	60.7
	Not Sure	36	12.0	12.6	73.3
	Less Interested	59	19.7	20.7	94.0
	Not Interested	17	5.7	6.0	100.0
Total		300	100.0		

Home Security

		Frequency	Percent	Valid Percent	Cumulative Percent
Valid	Very Interested	77	25.7	27.1	27.1
	Interested	109	36.3	38.4	65.5
	Not Sure	44	14.7	15.5	81.0
	Less Interested	39	13.0	13.7	94.7
	Not Interested	15	5.0	5.3	100.0
Total		300	100.0		

Automobiles

		Frequency	Percent	Valid Percent	Cumulative Percent
Valid	Very Interested	67	22.3	23.5	23.5
	Interested	99	33.0	34.7	58.2
	Not Sure	26	8.7	9.1	67.4
	Less Interested	63	21.0	22.1	89.5
	Not Interested	30	10.0	10.5	100.0
Total		300	100.0		

Health and Fitness

		Frequency	Percent	Valid Percent	Cumulative Percent
Valid	Yes	211	70.3	74.0	74.0
	No	74	24.7	26.0	100.0
	Total	285	95.0	100.0	
Total		300	100.0		

Home Appliances

		Frequency	Percent	Valid Percent	Cumulative Percent
Valid	Yes	189	63.0	66.3	66.3
	No	96	32.0	33.7	100.0
	Total	285	95.0	100.0	
Total		300	100.0		

Home Security

		Frequency	Percent	Valid Percent	Cumulative Percent
Valid	Yes	164	54.7	58.0	58.0
	No	119	39.7	42.0	100.0
	Total	283	94.3	100.0	
Total		300	100.0		

Automobiles

		Frequency	Percent	Valid Percent	Cumulative Percent
Valid	Yes	192	64.0	67.8	67.8
	No	91	30.3	32.2	100.0
	Total	283	94.3	100.0	
Total		300	100.0		

Descriptive Statistics

	N	Minimum	Maximum	Mean	Std. Deviation
Indicate your nationality.	300	.00	2.00	1.1967	.66291
Indicate your gender.	300	1.00	2.00	1.4667	.49972
I am familiar with the term Internet of things (IoT)	290	1.00	3.00	1.5138	.73575
How many devices connectable to the internet do I own?	290	1.00	4.00	1.7138	.81772
All my devices connectable to the internet are secure.	290	1.00	5.00	2.6828	.81256
I regularly update all my devices connectable to the internet.	289	1.00	5.00	2.1419	.95957
More work should be done by the IT industry and the government to educate consumers about internet security.	289	1.00	5.00	1.5363	.76346
I take protective measures around technological products (For example covering the camera on my laptop)	286	1.00	3.00	2.0035	.68824
I am discouraged from buying connectable devices due to security and privacy concerns	286	1.00	5.00	3.1434	1.06148
When using applications or devices connectable to the internet I am careful about giving out personal information.	286	1.00	5.00	1.8357	.88114
I think there is enough media coverage of attacks involving hacking and security breaches with regards to the Internet.	286	1.00	5.00	2.7832	1.05391
I think trust in technology by the consumers has decreased over time.	286	1.00	5.00	2.6643	1.06256
I would be willing to pay extra for a technological product that has better security	285	1.00	5.00	2.2772	.98421
Security	284	1.00	5.00	1.8380	.91038
Cost	285	1.00	5.00	1.7439	.75597
Features	285	1.00	5.00	1.5825	.71531

Brand	285	1.00	5.00	3.0526	1.21350
I would be willing to give out more personal information in exchange for better value offered:	285	1.00	5.00	3.2386	1.04776
Health and Fitness	285	1.00	5.00	2.5544	1.21668
Home Appliances	285	1.00	5.00	2.5614	1.15700
Home Security	284	1.00	5.00	2.3169	1.16407
Automobiles	285	1.00	5.00	2.6140	1.33683
Health and Fitness	285	1.00	2.00	1.2596	.43921
Home Appliances	285	1.00	2.00	1.3368	.47346
Home Security	283	1.00	2.00	1.4205	.49451
Automobiles	283	1.00	2.00	1.3216	.46790
Valid N (listwise)	281				

T-Test (Consumer Awareness)

Group Statistics

	Indicate your gender.	N	Mean	Std. Deviation
I am familiar with the term Internet of things (IoT)	Male	155	1.3806	.67680
	Female	135	1.6667	.77267
How many devices connectable to the internet do I own?	Male	155	1.8774	.87040
	Female	135	1.5259	.71058
All my devices connectable to the internet are secure.	Male	155	2.7355	.90509
	Female	135	2.6222	.68965
I regularly update all my devices connectable to the internet.	Male	154	1.9416	.87997
	Female	135	2.3704	.99806

More work should be done by the IT industry and the government to educate consumers about internet security.	Male	155	1.6258	.83859
	Female	134	1.4328	.65405

Group Statistics

	Indicate your gender.	Std. Error Mean
I am familiar with the term Internet of things (IoT)	Male	.05436
	Female	.06650
How many devices connectable to the internet do I own?	Male	.06991
	Female	.06116
All my devices connectable to the internet are secure.	Male	.07270
	Female	.05936
I regularly update all my devices connectable to the internet.	Male	.07091
	Female	.08590
More work should be done by the IT industry and the government to educate consumers about internet security.	Male	.06736
	Female	.05650

Independent Samples Test

		Levene's Test for Equality of Variances		t-test for Equality of Means
		F	Sig.	t
I am familiar with the term Internet of things (IoT)	Equal variances assumed	10.095	.002	-3.360
	Equal variances not assumed			-3.330

How many devices connectable to the internet do I own?	Equal variances assumed	7.037	.008	3.732
	Equal variances not assumed			3.784
All my devices connectable to the internet are secure.	Equal variances assumed	10.305	.001	1.185
	Equal variances not assumed			1.207
I regularly update all my devices connectable to the internet.	Equal variances assumed	8.425	.004	-3.882
	Equal variances not assumed			-3.850
More work should be done by the IT industry and the government to educate consumers about internet security.	Equal variances assumed	5.982	.015	2.156
	Equal variances not assumed			2.195

Independent Samples Test

		t-test for Equality of Means		
		df	Sig. (2-tailed)	Mean Difference
I am familiar with the term Internet of things (IoT)	Equal variances assumed	288	.001	-.28602
	Equal variances not assumed	268.573	.001	-.28602
How many devices connectable to the internet do I own?	Equal variances assumed	288	.000	.35149
	Equal variances not assumed	286.835	.000	.35149
All my devices connectable to the internet are secure.	Equal variances assumed	288	.237	.11326
	Equal variances not assumed	283.148	.229	.11326
I regularly update all my devices connectable to the internet.	Equal variances assumed	287	.000	-.42881
	Equal variances not assumed	269.320	.000	-.42881

More work should be done by the IT industry and the government to educate consumers about internet security.	Equal variances assumed	287	.032	.19297
	Equal variances not assumed	284.099	.029	.19297

Independent Samples Test

		t-test for Equality of Means	
		Std. Error Difference	95% Confidence Interval of the Difference
			Lower
I am familiar with the term Internet of things (IoT)	Equal variances assumed	.08511	-.45355
	Equal variances not assumed	.08589	-.45513
How many devices connectable to the internet do I own?	Equal variances assumed	.09418	.16612
	Equal variances not assumed	.09289	.16867
All my devices connectable to the internet are secure.	Equal variances assumed	.09559	-.07488
	Equal variances not assumed	.09385	-.07147
I regularly update all my devices connectable to the internet.	Equal variances assumed	.11047	-.64625
	Equal variances not assumed	.11139	-.64811
More work should be done by the IT industry and the government to educate consumers about internet security.	Equal variances assumed	.08949	.01683
	Equal variances not assumed	.08792	.01992

Independent Samples Test

		t-test for Equality of Means 95% Confidence Interval of the Difference Upper
I am familiar with the term Internet of things (IoT)	Equal variances assumed	-.11850
	Equal variances not assumed	-.11691
How many devices connectable to the internet do I own?	Equal variances assumed	.53687
	Equal variances not assumed	.53432
All my devices connectable to the internet are secure.	Equal variances assumed	.30141
	Equal variances not assumed	.29800
I regularly update all my devices connectable to the internet.	Equal variances assumed	-.21138
	Equal variances not assumed	-.20951
More work should be done by the IT industry and the government to educate consumers about internet security.	Equal variances assumed	.36911
	Equal variances not assumed	.36602

T-Test (Perception of Privacy)

Group Statistics

	Indicate your gender.	N	Mean	Std. Deviation
I take protective measures around technological products (For example covering the camera on my laptop)	Male	152	2.0197	.70448
	Female	134	1.9851	.67149

I am discouraged from buying connectable devices due to security and privacy concerns	Male	152	3.2237	1.15201
	Female	134	3.0522	.94445
When using applications or devices connectable to the internet I am careful about giving out personal information.	Male	152	1.8158	.90927
	Female	134	1.8582	.85094
I think there is enough media coverage of attacks involving hacking and security breaches with regards to the Internet.	Male	152	2.7237	1.11698
	Female	134	2.8507	.97724
I think trust in technology by the consumers has decreased over time.	Male	152	2.8224	1.11642
	Female	134	2.4851	.97128

Group Statistics

	Indicate your gender.	Std. Error Mean
I take protective measures around technological products (For example covering the camera on my laptop)	Male	.05714
	Female	.05801
I am discouraged from buying connectable devices due to security and privacy concerns	Male	.09344
	Female	.08159
When using applications or devices connectable to the internet I am careful about giving out personal information.	Male	.07375
	Female	.07351
I think there is enough media coverage of attacks involving hacking and security breaches with regards to the Internet.	Male	.09060
	Female	.08442
I think trust in technology by the consumers has decreased over time.	Male	.09055
	Female	.08391

Independent Samples Test

		Levene's Test for Equality of Variances		t-test for Equality of Means
		F	Sig.	t
I take protective measures around technological products (For example covering the camera on my laptop)	Equal variances assumed	.658	.418	.424
	Equal variances not assumed			.426
I am discouraged from buying connectable devices due to security and privacy concerns	Equal variances assumed	12.076	.001	1.365
	Equal variances not assumed			1.382
When using applications or devices connectable to the internet I am careful about giving out personal information.	Equal variances assumed	1.447	.230	-.406
	Equal variances not assumed			-.407
I think there is enough media coverage of attacks involving hacking and security breaches with regards to the Internet.	Equal variances assumed	7.007	.009	-1.017
	Equal variances not assumed			-1.026
I think trust in technology by the consumers has decreased over time.	Equal variances assumed	3.292	.071	2.708
	Equal variances not assumed			2.732

Independent Samples Test

		t-test for Equality of Means		
		df	Sig. (2-tailed)	Mean Difference
I take protective measures around technological products (For example covering the camera on my laptop)	Equal variances assumed	284	.672	.03466
	Equal variances not assumed	282.256	.671	.03466
I am discouraged from buying connectable devices due to security and privacy concerns	Equal variances assumed	284	.173	.17145
	Equal variances not assumed	282.553	.168	.17145
When using applications or devices connectable to the internet I am careful about giving out personal information.	Equal variances assumed	284	.685	-.04242
	Equal variances not assumed	282.974	.684	-.04242
I think there is enough media coverage of attacks involving hacking and security breaches with regards to the Internet.	Equal variances assumed	284	.310	-.12706
	Equal variances not assumed	283.985	.306	-.12706
I think trust in technology by the consumers has decreased over time.	Equal variances assumed	284	.007	.33729
	Equal variances not assumed	283.954	.007	.33729

Independent Samples Test

	t-test for Equality of Means	
		95% Confidence Interval of the Difference
	Std. Error Difference	Lower

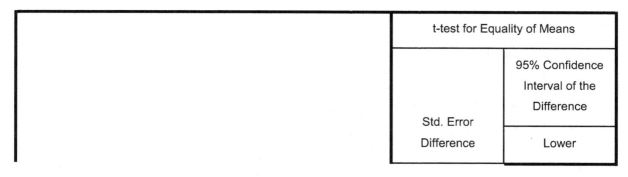

I take protective measures around technological products (For example covering the camera on my laptop)	Equal variances assumed	.08167	-.12610
	Equal variances not assumed	.08143	-.12562
I am discouraged from buying connectable devices due to security and privacy concerns	Equal variances assumed	.12559	-.07577
	Equal variances not assumed	.12405	-.07273
When using applications or devices connectable to the internet I am careful about giving out personal information.	Equal variances assumed	.10457	-.24824
	Equal variances not assumed	.10413	-.24739
I think there is enough media coverage of attacks involving hacking and security breaches with regards to the Internet.	Equal variances assumed	.12488	-.37287
	Equal variances not assumed	.12383	-.37081
I think trust in technology by the consumers has decreased over time.	Equal variances assumed	.12453	.09217
	Equal variances not assumed	.12345	.09430

Independent Samples Test

		t-test for Equality of Means
		95% Confidence Interval of the Difference
		Upper
I take protective measures around technological products (For example covering the camera on my laptop)	Equal variances assumed	.19542
	Equal variances not assumed	.19494
I am discouraged from buying connectable devices due to security and privacy concerns	Equal variances assumed	.41866
	Equal variances not assumed	.41562

When using applications or devices connectable to the internet I am careful about giving out personal information.	Equal variances assumed	.16340
	Equal variances not assumed	.16255
I think there is enough media coverage of attacks involving hacking and security breaches with regards to the Internet.	Equal variances assumed	.11874
	Equal variances not assumed	.11669
I think trust in technology by the consumers has decreased over time.	Equal variances assumed	.58242
	Equal variances not assumed	.58029

T-Test (Perception of Value)

Group Statistics

	Indicate your gender.	N	Mean	Std. Deviation
I would be willing to pay extra for a technological product that has better security	Male	152	2.2632	1.05941
	Female	133	2.2932	.89427
Security	Male	151	1.8212	.91714
	Female	133	1.8571	.90573
Cost	Male	152	1.7697	.77605
	Female	133	1.7143	.73414
Features	Male	152	1.4013	.57842
	Female	133	1.7895	.79822
Brand	Male	152	2.9145	1.22309
	Female	133	3.2105	1.18739
I would be willing to give out more personal information in exchange for better value offered:	Male	152	3.1711	1.16105
	Female	133	3.3158	.89923
Health and Fitness	Male	152	2.6382	1.24778
	Female	133	2.4586	1.17751

Home Appliances	Male	152	2.4211	1.12483
	Female	133	2.7218	1.17650
Home Security	Male	151	2.3311	1.14730
	Female	133	2.3008	1.18696
Automobiles	Male	152	2.2105	1.21596
	Female	133	3.0752	1.32359
Health and Fitness	Male	152	1.2961	.45802
	Female	133	1.2180	.41448
Home Appliances	Male	152	1.2763	.44865
	Female	133	1.4060	.49294
Home Security	Male	151	1.3510	.47887
	Female	132	1.5000	.50190
Automobiles	Male	152	1.2303	.42239
	Female	131	1.4275	.49661

Group Statistics

	Indicate your gender.	Std. Error Mean
I would be willing to pay extra for a technological product that has better security	Male	.08593
	Female	.07754
Security	Male	.07464
	Female	.07854
Cost	Male	.06295
	Female	.06366
Features	Male	.04692
	Female	.06921

Brand	Male	.09921
	Female	.10296
I would be willing to give out more personal information in exchange for better value offered:	Male	.09417
	Female	.07797
Health and Fitness	Male	.10121
	Female	.10210
Home Appliances	Male	.09124
	Female	.10202
Home Security	Male	.09337
	Female	.10292
Automobiles	Male	.09863
	Female	.11477
Health and Fitness	Male	.03715
	Female	.03594
Home Appliances	Male	.03639
	Female	.04274
Home Security	Male	.03897
	Female	.04369
Automobiles	Male	.03426
	Female	.04339

Independent Samples Test

	Levene's Test for Equality of Variances		t-test for Equality of Means			
	F	Sig.	t	df	Sig. (2-tailed)	Mean Difference

I would be willing to pay extra for a technological product that has better security	Equal variances assumed	1.396	.238	-.257	283	.797	-.03008
	Equal variances not assumed			-.260	282.648	.795	-.03008
Security	Equal variances assumed	.034	.854	-.332	282	.740	-.03595
	Equal variances not assumed			-.332	278.321	.740	-.03595
Cost	Equal variances assumed	.101	.751	.617	283	.538	.05545
	Equal variances not assumed			.619	281.264	.536	.05545
Features	Equal variances assumed	2.221	.137	-4.740	283	.000	-.38816
	Equal variances not assumed			-4.642	237.360	.000	-.38816
Brand	Equal variances assumed	1.510	.220	-2.067	283	.040	-.29605
	Equal variances not assumed			-2.071	279.943	.039	-.29605
I would be willing to give out more personal information in exchange for better value offered:	Equal variances assumed	9.718	.002	-1.164	283	.245	-.14474
	Equal variances not assumed			-1.184	279.003	.237	-.14474
Health and Fitness	Equal variances assumed	2.129	.146	1.244	283	.215	.17951
	Equal variances not assumed			1.249	281.370	.213	.17951
Home Appliances	Equal variances assumed	2.397	.123	-2.204	283	.028	-.30075

	Equal variances not assumed			-2.197	274.238	.029	-.30075
Home Security	Equal variances assumed	.621	.431	.219	282	.827	.03037
	Equal variances not assumed			.219	274.849	.827	.03037
Automobiles	Equal variances assumed	6.472	.011	-5.746	283	.000	-.86466
	Equal variances not assumed			-5.714	270.155	.000	-.86466
Health and Fitness	Equal variances assumed	9.243	.003	1.499	283	.135	.07801
	Equal variances not assumed			1.509	282.671	.132	.07801
Home Appliances	Equal variances assumed	18.889	.000	-2.325	283	.021	-.12970
	Equal variances not assumed			-2.310	269.110	.022	-.12970
Home Security	Equal variances assumed	12.775	.000	-2.553	281	.011	-.14901
	Equal variances not assumed			-2.545	272.014	.011	-.14901
Automobiles	Equal variances assumed	42.316	.000	-3.610	281	.000	-.19722
	Equal variances not assumed			-3.567	256.724	.000	-.19722

Independent Samples Test

	t-test for Equality of Means	
	Std. Error Difference	95% Confidence Interval of the Difference

			Lower	Upper
I would be willing to pay extra for a technological product that has better security	Equal variances assumed	.11705	-.26048	.20033
	Equal variances not assumed	.11574	-.25791	.19776
Security	Equal variances assumed	.10843	-.24939	.17749
	Equal variances not assumed	.10834	-.24923	.17733
Cost	Equal variances assumed	.08986	-.12142	.23232
	Equal variances not assumed	.08952	-.12077	.23167
Features	Equal variances assumed	.08189	-.54935	-.22696
	Equal variances not assumed	.08362	-.55288	-.22343
Brand	Equal variances assumed	.14326	-.57804	-.01406
	Equal variances not assumed	.14298	-.57750	-.01461
I would be willing to give out more personal information in exchange for better value offered:	Equal variances assumed	.12433	-.38946	.09999
	Equal variances not assumed	.12226	-.38541	.09594
Health and Fitness	Equal variances assumed	.14432	-.10457	.46359
	Equal variances not assumed	.14376	-.10348	.46250
Home Appliances	Equal variances assumed	.13645	-.56934	-.03216
	Equal variances not assumed	.13686	-.57018	-.03132
Home Security	Equal variances assumed	.13866	-.24257	.30332
	Equal variances not assumed	.13896	-.24319	.30394
Automobiles	Equal variances assumed	.15047	-1.16085	-.56848

	Equal variances not assumed	.15133	-1.16259	-.56673
Health and Fitness	Equal variances assumed	.05204	-.02442	.18043
	Equal variances not assumed	.05169	-.02374	.17975
Home Appliances	Equal variances assumed	.05578	-.23951	-.01989
	Equal variances not assumed	.05614	-.24022	-.01918
Home Security	Equal variances assumed	.05836	-.26388	-.03414
	Equal variances not assumed	.05854	-.26426	-.03376
Automobiles	Equal variances assumed	.05463	-.30475	-.08969
	Equal variances not assumed	.05528	-.30609	-.08835

www.ingramcontent.com/pod-product-compliance
Lightning Source LLC
LaVergne TN
LVHW082347060326
832902LV00017B/2707